CYCLING VANCOUVER ISLAND

JOHN CROUCH

Cycling VANCOUVER *Island*

RMB

For information on purchasing bulk quantities of this book, or to obtain media excerpts or invite the author to speak at an event, please visit rmbooks.com and select the "Contact" tab.

RMB | Rocky Mountain Books Ltd.
rmbooks.com
@rmbooks
facebook.com/rmbooks

Cataloguing data available from Library and Archives Canada
ISBN 9781771605618 (print)
ISBN 9781771605625 (electronic)

All photographs are by John Crouch unless otherwise noted.
Cover photo: iStock.com/MarkMalleson

Printed and bound in China

We would like to also take this opportunity to acknowledge the traditional territories upon which we live and work. In Calgary, Alberta, we acknowledge the Niitsítapi (Blackfoot) and the people of the Treaty 7 region in Southern Alberta, which includes the Siksika, the Piikuni, the Kainai, the Tsuut'ina and the Stoney Nakoda First Nations, including Chiniki, Bearpaw, and Wesley First Nations. The City of Calgary is also home to Métis Nation of Alberta, Region III. In Victoria, British Columbia, we acknowledge the traditional territories of the Lkwungen (Esquimalt, and Songhees), Malahat, Pacheedaht, Scia'new, T'Sou-ke and W̱SÁNEĆ (Pauquachin, Tsartlip, Tsawout, Tseycum) peoples.

We acknowledge the financial support of the Government of Canada through the Canada Book Fund and the Canada Council for the Arts, and of the province of British Columbia through the British Columbia Arts Council and the Book Publishing Tax Credit.

Disclaimer

The actions described in this book may be considered inherently dangerous activities. Individuals undertake these activities at their own risk. The information put forth in this guide has been collected from a variety of sources and is not guaranteed to be completely accurate or reliable. Many conditions and some information may change owing to weather and numerous other factors beyond the control of the authors and publishers. Individuals or groups must determine the risks, use their own judgment, and take full responsibility for their actions. Do not depend on any information found in this book for your own personal safety. Your safety depends on your own good judgment based on your skills, education, and experience. It is up to the users of this guidebook to acquire the necessary skills for safe experiences and to exercise caution in potentially hazardous areas. The authors and publishers of this guide accept no responsibility for your actions or the results that occur from another's actions, choices, or judgments. If you have any doubt as to your safety or your ability to attempt anything described in this guidebook, do not attempt it.

For Leo, Jeffrey and Gabor.

Contents

Introduction

He wasn't the first European to set eyes on Vancouver Island – not by a long shot – but Sir James Douglas was the first to exclaim that it was "a perfect Eden" when almost two hundred years ago he saw the southern reaches of the island on the edge of the Pacific Ocean that you're about to discover for yourself. (Douglas became the first governor of British Columbia, in 1858.)

Of course, whether you agree with Douglas or not would depend on whether you share the same notion of Eden as he had, but I'll wager you'll be pretty impressed by what you see and experience as you cycle the roads and trails of this, the largest island on the west coast of North America.

Geographically the Island is a place of contrasts, often stark: where mountains meet ocean on the rugged west coast; where forest gives way to fertile, expansive river valleys as in the Cowichan, Alberni and Comox valleys; or where the coastline becomes fragmented into a filigree of small islands.

Fortunately, due to the creation of myriad parks, the Island's diverse ecosystems that define the land have been protected. Nevertheless, in a park or not, you're never far away from a river or creek, a lake or hilly terrain or a long stretch of beach. Farmland, meadows, marshes, hills, rainforests and mountains are all, in some measure, encompassed in this book's routes up and down the Island.

With the understanding you're not going to cycle the Island all in one go, this guidebook is divided into sections that roughly correspond to the Island's geographic and population regions. Obviously, the more populated a region the larger the network of roads. That's why the southern part of the

Island has the most route descriptions – it's the most populated. That's not to imply the middle and northern parts of the Island are not represented. They are. But not to the same degree. To compensate, the longest route in the book takes you from the Island's southern tip (Victoria) to the north Island's largest settlement, Port Hardy, a more than 500km/310mi journey that passes through all the main settlements on the Island's east side.

But each section has its own allure. The south has the province's capital, Victoria, to discover along with the Highlands, the Saanich Peninsula, Metchosin and the craggy shores of East Sooke's headlands. Just west of Victoria are Sooke, Jordan River and Port Renfrew, accessed along the West Coast Highway. North of the famous (some might say "infamous") Malahat Drive is the Cowichan Valley, renowned for its vineyards and summer sunshine. Nanaimo, farther north, is a major portal to the island from Vancouver and serves as a bustling centre for the mid- to upper-island communities. The Comox Valley is a hive both of winter and summer activities. Its proximity to Mt. Washington and the splendid Strathcona Provincial Park makes it a destination for skiing and snowboarding in winter and hiking and climbing in summer. The valley's communities of Courtenay, Comox and Cumberland have artistic and cultural events that belie their relatively modest size. Campbell River, an erstwhile forestry and pulp mill town, is now known for being the "salmon capital of the world" and all that that title entails, i.e., tourism, lodges and access to the water. It's also the junction of highways 19, 19A and 28, the latter going to Gold River via Upper Campbell Lake, Buttle Lake and Strathcona Park. The ferry to the islands of Quadra and Cortes depart from its downtown. The road to Port Hardy passes through Campbell River, a little over halfway between Victoria and Port Hardy.

The island wasn't always called Vancouver Island. No, it had a slightly more complicated name. Here's what happened. Because the Spanish, under the leadership of Bodega y Quadra, had explored the Island some years before the British sailor George Vancouver began charting the area, they thought they had prior claim. But it was a testament to the friendship that grew between Quadra and Vancouver as they joined forces to explore and chart the vast territory, that in 1792 during ownership negotiations, Vancouver suggested calling the island Quadra and Vancouver Island (some sources say Quadra's and Vancouver's Island). Over time, as Spanish interest in the area diminished, so did the use of Quadra's name. By the early 1800s, as the commercial activity of the British Hudson's Bay Company increased on the island, Vancouver Island became its only name.

The original intent of both the Spanish and the British in plying the waters of the Pacific Northwest was not colonization but the discovery and establishing of a northwest passage between the Pacific and Atlantic oceans. The passage, if found, would facilitate a lucrative trade between Europe and the Far East. In the process, any resources they came across on the lands they encountered could be traded for. That's what happened on Vancouver Island. In fact, trade became more important than finding the Northwest Passage. Both nations (initiated by the Russians) began trading with (some would say "exploiting") the island's Indigenous people for the furs they offered. In a matter of a few years, the sea otter population of the Island's waters was decimated. Other species such as marten, beaver, raccoon, bear and lynx were also prized by the Europeans and also suffered.

It was this trading impulse that propelled the Hudson's Bay Company's Sir James Douglas into exploring the whole

Island for its riches. By ship at first and then primarily overland, during the mid- to late-1800s, men were sent to search for routes by which trade could flourish and expand. Often led by First Nations guides, these men followed ancient trails and routes that have, over the last century and a half, morphed into many of the roads we travel today.

Of course, Indigenous peoples have lived on the Island for millennia, having crossed the land bridge between Siberia and Alaska with others who migrated throughout the Americas. These First Nations are distinguished by their languages and where they live on the island. The Kwakwaka'wakw nation live in the northern part of the Island, with Alert Bay, on Cormorant Island a few kilometres by water from Port McNeill, being one of its main centres. Farther north, Port Hardy and the neighbouring Fort Rupert are other centres. Campbell River and Quadra Island are other important Kwakwaka'wakw communities. All these communities can be visited on the longest ride in the book (route 43, Victoria to Port Hardy, p261).

The first of the Island's Indigenous peoples to come into contact with Europeans were the Nuu-chah-nulth. The most famous of those encounters was in 1778 between the Nuu-chah-nulth chief Maquinna and the English explorer James Cook. Maquinna was a master of commerce and met with many European traders (including Bodega y Quadra and George Vancouver) to barter animal pelts for metal goods. James Cook made a major linguistic blooper when, entering Nuu-chah-nulth waters for the first time, he misunderstood welcoming Nuu-chah-nulth paddlers who shouted from their canoe, "Itchme, nutka! Itchme nutka!" which meant "Go around! Go around!" Cook thought they were introducing themselves as the "Nootka." The name stuck until recently when the Nuu-chah-nulth asserted the use of their linguistically correct name. Nootka is still used in place names for Nootka Island and Nootka Sound. The Nuu-chah-nulth traditional lands are on the island's west coast. Their principal communities are accessible by bike such as Gold River, Tofino, Ucluelet and Port Alberni.

By far the largest population of Indigenous people on the island are the Coast Salish, comprising many First Nations, including the Snuneymuxw, Stz'uminus, Tsartlip, Tseycum, Tsawout, Malahat and T'Sou-ke, to name only a few. Their traditional lands stretch the length of much of the Salish Sea, from Comox and Courtenay in the north to Sooke, Port Renfrew, the Saanich Peninsula, Esquimalt and Victoria in the south. In between are Nanaimo, Ladysmith, Chemainus, Duncan, the Cowichan Valley and Mill Bay. All are visited in one or more of the book's routes.

With this glimpse into the Island's past and present, perhaps its future will be to welcome you, on your bike – along with others (if you choose) – to explore, to enjoy and to fully savour all that the Island has to offer.

Getting to the Island

There are numerous portals to Vancouver Island, by ferry and by air.

Ferries

TSAWWASSEN (VANCOUVER) TO SWARTZ BAY (VICTORIA)

This ferry route connects BC's Lower Mainland to southern Vancouver Island. The Tsawwassen terminal is 36 kilometres (22 miles) due south from downtown Vancouver. The Swartz Bay terminal is 32 kilometres (20 miles) north of Victoria. The sailing time is about 1 hour and 30 minutes. (See Ferry and Airport Routes A at p313 for directions to downtown Victoria.)

PORT ANGELES (WASHINGTON STATE) TO VICTORIA

The MV *Coho*, a ferry run by the private company Black Ball Ferry Line, operates four times a day during the summer months from downtown Port Angeles to downtown Victoria. The sailing time is 1 hour and 30 minutes. (Turn left out of the terminal for downtown Victoria.)

VESUVIUS (SALT SPRING ISLAND) TO CROFTON

This is a convenient route for travellers coming to Vancouver Island from the Gulf Islands. It's short (25 minutes) and lands about 15 kilometres (9 miles) northeast of Duncan. (Coming off the ferry, follow the signage for Maple Bay or Duncan if going south or for Nanaimo if going north.)

HORSESHOE BAY (VANCOUVER) TO DEPARTURE BAY (NANAIMO)

There are two ferry routes from the Lower Mainland to Nanaimo. The shortest and quickest is from Horseshoe Bay, 20 kilometres (12 miles) northwest of Vancouver, to Nanaimo's Departure Bay, a voyage of 1 hour and 40 minutes. (See Ferry and Airport Access Route D on p321 for directions north and south from terminal.)

TSAWWASSEN TO DUKE POINT (NANAIMO)

Duke Point is 16 kilometres (9 miles) south of Nanaimo. This is a convenient route for travellers coming from south of Vancouver. The sailing time is 2 hours. (See Ferry and Airport Access Routes A on p313 for directions north and south from terminal.)

POWELL RIVER TO COMOX

For those travellers coming to the Island from the northern part of the Sunshine Coast this ferry is the most convenient route. It runs four times a day and takes 1 hour and 30 minutes. (From the terminal, follow the signage for Courtenay and Highway 19 to go south or north.)

bcferries.com

cohoferry.com

Airports

VICTORIA INTERNATIONAL AIRPORT (YYJ)

This airport is situated about 25 kilometres (15 miles) north of Victoria. The airport has a bike assembly station with tools and a pump plus storage lockers. There is limited public transportation to downtown Victoria. Unless your bike is boxed, the shuttle and taxi options are not usually available to cyclists. (See Ferry and Airport Access Route E, p323, for directions to downtown Victoria.)

victoriaairport.com

NANAIMO AIRPORT (YCD)

The airport is 18 kilometres (11 miles) south of Nanaimo and 9 kilometres (6 miles) north of Ladysmith. It's situated on Highway 1, the Trans-Canada, so exiting and directions north and south are straightforward.

nanaimoairport.com

COMOX VALLEY AIRPORT (YQQ)

Located about 10 kilometres (6 miles) northeast of downtown Courtenay, this airport is, essentially, part of CFB Comox. Turn R on exiting the airport and follow the signs for either Comox, Courtenay or Highway 19 (for north and south), depending on your itinerary.

comoxairport.com

Climate

Vancouver Island has the mildest climate in the whole

country. That said, precipitation and temperatures do vary from south to north and from east to west of the Island – in winter and summer. The following is what it looks like from June to September, on average.

The South Island, i.e., from Nanaimo south to Victoria, has the mildest and driest conditions on the Island. Summer temperatures can get as high as 28 to 30°C (82.4 to 86.0°F), with Victoria's annual precipitation as low as 608 mm (23.9 inches). The average summer temperature is 18 to 20°C (64.4 to 68°F), while rainfall averages 18.3 mm (0.72 inch).

North of Nanaimo to the tip of the Island average summer temperatures range from 14°C (57.2°F) in Port Hardy to 20.5°C (69°F) in Courtenay. Average summer rainfall is 60 mm (2.4 inches) for Port Hardy and 25 mm (1 inch) for Courtenay.

The largest disparity in rain and warmth throughout the year is between the east and west of the Island. The east side is drier and warmer than the west. For example, at Tofino on the west coast the average summer temperature is 14.2°C (57.5°F). At Parksville on the east coast it is 20.2°C (72.0°F). Tofino's average rainfall is 92 mm (3.6 inches), while Parksville gets only 40 mm (1.6 inches) – quite a difference.

How to use this guide

All the route descriptions follow a similar scheme. Often there is a short introduction intended to summarize what you're likely to see and experience while on the ride. The introduction is also intended to whet your appetite for the ride rather than give every detail. The Island's communities and roads are for you to discover and explore. Too much information from me might interfere with that. (I have included links to informative websites for a number of areas.)

The descriptions include the following categories.

DISTANCE

Because the book describes routes that are intended to be used both by Canadians and by riders from the United States, measurements are given in each country's official system: kilometres for Canada, miles for the US. (The conversion formula is 1 kilometre = 0.6 mile; 1 mile = 1.6 kilometres.)

LEVEL

This, of course, indicates the degree of difficulty of a route. For some riders this is the most important piece of information in the whole book. Though not described in detail, the three designations – Easy, Moderate and Strenuous – will, I hope, enable you to choose routes you can accomplish without too much discomfort. Remember, though, you're often cycling on terrain that is inherently hilly, and even though a route might be described as easy, it will inevitably have some variation in elevation along its course.

HIGHLIGHTS

These are places, buildings, roads, sites, parks, views, beaches etc. which I think might appeal to riders as they tour the Island's communities and roads.

START

This is the location of the route's start and, in some instances, because a route is a loop, its finish.

THE ROUTES

I've used what I think is a simple and easy-to-comprehend format. First there is the checkpoint number, e.g., 4. Then follows the distance from the route's start in kilometres and miles in brackets, e.g., (7.5km/4.6mi). This is followed by a written description of the route. The checkpoints correspond with those on the accompanying map. It's always a good idea to compare what you're reading with what you're seeing on the map. The directional "right" and "left" are rendered as R and L.

SAFE CYCLING

The first principle of cycling on roads, to my mind, is to behave as if you belong there. And you do. But what does that mean, exactly? Well, it means:

- riding according to the rules of the road (see below);
- riding confidently and with good bike-handling skills;
- giving good, clear hand signals;
- making eye contact with vehicle drivers, other cyclists and pedestrians at intersections and driveways;
- riding defensively and with awareness of what is going on around you; and
- riding conspicuously, i.e., wearing bright colours and reflective clothing.

According to Part 3 of British Columbia's Motor Vehicle Act (RSBC 1996, c. 318), a cyclist has the same rights and duties as a driver of a motor vehicle. Here are some other requirements of the Act as it pertains to cyclists.

A cyclist:

- must not ride on a sidewalk unless directed by official signage;
- must ride as near as practicable to the right side of the road except when turning left or overtaking;
- must not ride two abreast on the roadway;
- is not required to ride on any part of a road that is not paved;
- must use lights – white in front, red in back – during hours of darkness;
- must have good brakes; and
- must wear a safety-approved helmet properly fitted and securely fastened.

Readers can find a more complete version of the Motor Vehicle Act at the BC Cycling Coalition webpage "Cycling and the Law," at bccc.bc.ca/bikesense-index/cycling-and-the-law.

MAP LEGEND

Land

Park

Water

Inset

Route

Ferry route

Road

Border

Route direction

S Start marker

F Finish marker

S·F Start/Finish marker

1 Route reference marker

Camping

Airport

Ferry terminal

Café / Restaurant

Landmark

PART ONE: VICTORIA

Though not the largest city in the province (Vancouver has that spot – by a long way) it is certainly the most attractive, not only from an architectural point of view but from a geographical one. The city is at the southern end of a peninsula – the Saanich Peninsula – and as such, is surrounded by water. That water is the Salish Sea. And the two constituent parts of that larger body of water that cuddle Victoria are the Strait of Juan de Fuca and Haro Strait. These straits give spectacular views of the Olympic Mountains and the San Juan Islands, to the south and east respectively.

The city itself has a population of well under a hundred thousand (Greater Victoria swells that number almost four-fold) and is nicely compact to allow easy walking and cycling to all of its examples of early 20th century architecture, its numerous nooks and crannies and the park and inner harbour that give the city its charm and appeal.

The architecture I'm referring to is that of Francis Rattenbury, the rascally Brit who designed and built the Empress Hotel, the BC legislature buildings and the CPR steamship terminal, all three edging the Inner Harbour. (For Vancouverites, you'll be familiar with Rattenbury's work in his design of the Vancouver courthouse, now the city's art gallery.) On the eastern edge of town are Craigdarroch Castle, the coal baron Robert Dunsmuir's attempt at emulating a Scottish baronial castle and now a museum, and Government House with its delightful mix of formal and not-so-formal gardens and Garry oak meadows.

In the heart of old Victoria are Market Square and Chinatown. Both have intriguing cubbyhole spaces, the most famous of which is Fan Tan Alley. At just over a metre wide and a short block in length, the alley is regarded as Canada's narrowest street.

The Inner Harbour and its causeway is a tourist haven (if you want one). Buskers abound, and so of course do water-craft of all shapes and sizes. The steamship terminal is also here and is now an art gallery and restaurant.

To the south of downtown (and at the butt end of Douglas Street, aka the Trans-Canada Highway) is Beacon Hill Park. It creatively combines formal gardens; small lakes; wild, treed hill slopes; lawns; a cricket pitch and a children's farm into a place that pleases just about everyone.

For more on Victoria and Greater Victoria see tourismvictoria.com.

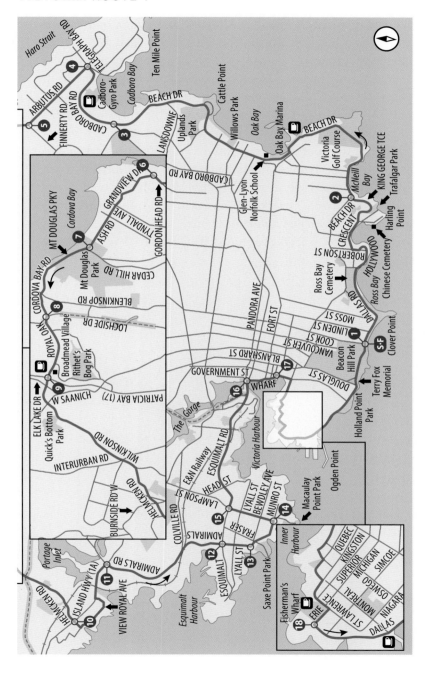

Tour of Victoria

Set on the rocky shores of a peninsula that juts into the confluence of two large bodies of water of the Salish Sea – the Strait of Juan de Fuca and Haro Strait – Victoria and its most famous (and oldest) park, Beacon Hill, is the ideal place to start and end a grand circle of the neighbourhoods that comprise Greater Victoria.

Endowed with a stunning location, Beacon Hill Park typifies the exceptional environments Victoria has to offer. From its formal gardens, its windswept Garry oaks, its totem pole and its two-kilometre-long (1.2 mile) clifftop walkway plus the magnificent views south over the ocean to the mountains of the Olympic Peninsula, the park seems to have everything.

On the ride you follow the Victoria shoreline going east. You pass Ross Bay Cemetery, and after Crescent Road you enter Oak Bay along its scenic Beach Drive. The ride down the hill into Cadboro Bay Village is your entry into the municipality of Saanich (the largest on the island). Next is the Gordon Head neighbourhood, and after riding along the eastern edge of the forested Mount Douglas Park you enter Broadmead, a large, carefully planned community.

You cross the Pat Bay Highway to head southwest along Wilkinson Road, and after passing Victoria General Hospital on your left, you cross the Trans-Canada Highway and ride through the streets of View Royal. The dockyards of the Naden naval base are next, a sign that you're now in the municipality of Esquimalt. Because of its favourable harbour, the British Navy, when they saw this place in 1865, decided to make Esquimalt the permanent naval base for its Pacific fleet. It's now, of course, solely Canadian.

A favourite oceanside park is Esquimalt's Saxe Point Park. Named for Queen Victoria's consort, Prince Albert, whose family name was Saxe-Coburg-Gotha, Saxe Point is just one of three municipal parks along this jagged shoreline.

Your entry back into the city of Victoria proper is via the Johnson Street Bridge (a bascule-type structure) and the Inner Harbour surrounded on two sides by grand architecture of the Victorian era: the Empress Hotel and the legislative buildings. Although the charm and grandeur of these buildings is a hard act to follow, your finish in Beacon Hill Park will reassure you that Mother Nature (with a little help) is not to be outdone.

DISTANCE	47km/29mi.
LEVEL	Easy to moderate.
HIGHLIGHTS	Beacon Hill Park; Oak Bay Marina; Cadboro Bay Village; Mount Douglas Park; Saxe Point Park; Victoria's Inner Harbour; Fisherman's Wharf and James Bay's Ogden Point.
START	Follow Douglas Street (Trans-Canada Hwy 1) south toward the ocean and the "Mile 0" monument. Turn L onto Dallas Road in Beacon Hill Park. Park on the R opposite the totem pole 100m/yd before the Cook Street intersection.

The route

① From the Dallas Road parking area, ride east, passing Clover Point R and Ross Bay Cemetery L. Dallas becomes Hollywood Crescent. After 2.8km/1.7mi turn R off Hollywood onto Crescent Road, which soon bears L to become the steep King George Terrace.

② (4.5km/2.8mi) At the stop sign at the bottom of King George Terrace Turn R onto Beach Drive. Continue on Beach, passing Oak Bay Marina, and on through the select neighbourhood of the Uplands.

③ (12.4km/7.7mi)   At the northern gates of the Uplands continue on what is now Cadboro Bay Road. Ride through the village as the road winds towards Ten Mile Point.

④ (14.1km/8.8mi)   Turn L onto Arbutus Road at a four-way stop.

⑤ (15.9km9.9mi)   Turn R at a three-way stop onto a continuation of Arbutus.

⑥ (17.0km/10.5mi)   Turn R onto Gordon Head Road. (At a sharp L bend Gordon Head becomes Ferndale, which in turn becomes Grandview Drive as Ferndale goes to the R. Stay on Grandview, which becomes Ash Road at the next four-way stop. Continue on Ash until it intersects Cordova Bay Road.

⑦ (20.3km/12.6mi)   Turn R onto Cordova Bay Road (aka Mount Douglas Parkway). The entrance to Mount Douglas Park's carpark/picnic area is just past this junction, on the R.

⑧ (22.7km/14.1mi)   At the four-way traffic light continue straight, onto Royal Oak Drive.

⑨ (25.1km/15.6mi)   With the Broadmead Village Shopping Centre on your L, cross the Pat Bay Highway on the overpass. Continue through three lighted intersections onto Wilkinson Road (at the West Saanich Road intersection). Wilkinson eventually becomes Helmcken Road shortly after its intersection with Interurban Road. At 31km/19mi you'll cross the Trans-Canada Highway and continue on a narrower but safe section of Helmcken Road.

⑩	(32.3km/20.1mi)	At the next light cross the Old Island Highway and continue on Helmcken, riding down to the junction with View Royal Avenue. Turn L onto View Royal and follow it as it snakes to its junction with the Old Island Highway. Turn R here.
⑪	(33.8km/23.7mi)	Turn R onto Admirals Road. Admirals Walk Shopping Centre is on the R.
⑫	(36.7km/22.8mi)	After passing the Naden naval base on the R you cross Esquimalt Road in the town centre and continue on Admirals.
⑬	(37.7km/23.4mi)	Turn briefly onto Bewdley (the entrance to Saxe Point Park is a few metres/yards on the R), crossing Fraser Street onto Munro Street.
⑭	(38.1km/23.7mi)	Passing the Fleming Beach boat launch and Buxton Green Park on your R, turn L onto Lampson Street.
⑮	(39.0km/24.2mi)	Turn R onto Esquimalt Road. You'll ride on this road back into Victoria, crossing the Johnson Street Bridge.
⑯	(42.0km/26.1mi)	Just over the bridge turn R into the bike lane of Wharf Street.
⑰	(42.7 km/26.5mi)	Turn R onto Government Street at the art deco Victoria Tourism building and then, after passing in front of the Empress Hotel, turn R onto Belleville Street. (The BC Legislature is on your L.) You now encounter a series of short streets that follows the coastline.
⑱	(44.0km/27.3mi)	Pass Fisherman's Wharf on St. Lawrence Street and, as you join

Dallas Road, the cruise ship terminal, a café and the Ogden Point breakwater, all on your R. Continue on Dallas back to Beacon Hill Park and your starting point.

Top: *Wildlife in Ross Bay Cemetery.*
Bottom: *Ross Bay along Dallas Road.*

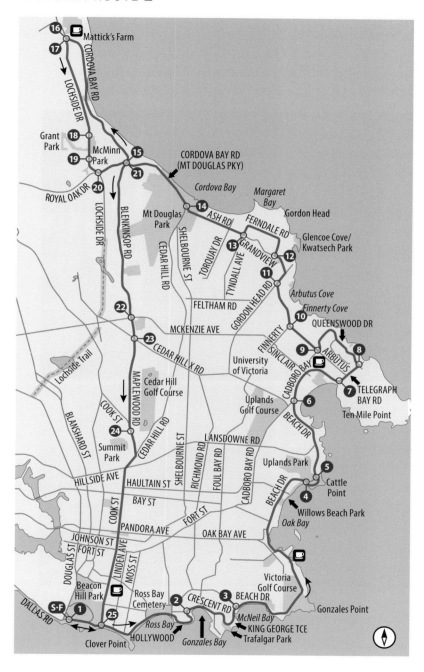

Coastline Cruise

On a warm summer's morning when the air is fresh, the mountains are clear as a bell and the sun is glinting off a rippling ocean, it's hard not to contemplate a ride along Victoria's stunning coastline. Nothing could be grander. And the added bonuses of the ride are numerous, including many viewpoints and rest stops along the way.

One might suppose that a coastal route would be flat as a pancake. Well, in Victoria that's not so, as your first viewpoint will attest. It's atop King George Terrace, about 4km/2.5mi into the ride. Your ride up the short but steep hill will be rewarded with a spectacular view over the Strait of Juan de Fuca to the Olympic Mountains and the San Juan Islands to the left. Below are Trial Island, Harling Point and the Chinese Cemetery, which, incidentally, was meant only as a temporary resting place until the local Chinese community could send the deceased back to their homeland.

Oak Bay's marina is one of three spots to rest and replenish in the first part of the ride. The other two are Willows Park (and beach) and the village of Cadboro Bay. After Cadboro Bay you ride through the Queenswood neighbourhood along a surprisingly tranquil and wooded road that twists amongst large homes with equally large gardens. Just before you begin the long curve of Cordova Bay you'll ride through the eastern edge of one of Victoria's favourite parks – Mount Douglas Park. Its entrance on the R leads to the park's beach and picnic area, which are very accessible.

Mattick's Farm with its stores and café is a great spot to end any bike ride. As you'll notice, I've suggested a couple of routes back to Beacon Hill Park. You can, of course, call a taxi, or a friend, and get chauffeured back.

DISTANCE	28km/17.5mi – one way. 56km/35mi – out and back. 44km/27mi – loop.
LEVEL	Moderate.
HIGHLIGHTS	Spectacular ocean views; numerous rest stops; parks; secluded neighbourhoods; little traffic; few crossroads except on the routes back.
START	From downtown take Douglas Street south (toward the ocean). Beacon Hill Park is on your L after the Southgate Street intersection. Bear L just before Douglas intersects Dallas Road (in the centre grassy area is the "Mile 0" sign and the Terry Fox statue). Continue east on Dallas for about 150 metres/yards to the Beacon Hill historical sign on your R. There is ample parking along the road.

The route

①   From the parking area along Dallas Road in front of the "Beacon Hill" historical information sign, start your ride going east along Dallas Road, i.e., away from the Douglas Street intersection. (At 2km/1.2mi you'll pass Ross Bay Cemetery on your L.)

② (3.0km/1.9mi)   Turn R onto Ross Street. (The entrance to Gonzales Bay beach is 30m/yd on the R.) Ross continues as Crescent Road. At 3.8km/2.4mi the steep but short hill of King George Terrace begins. Trafalgar Park Lookout is at the crest of the hill. Harling Point is below.

③ (4.9km/3.0mi)   At a stop sign, turn R onto Beach Drive (McNeill Bay begins here). There follows a series of interesting locations until checkpoint 4:

- 6.3 km Victoria Golf Course

- 7.5 km Oak Bay Beach Hotel (The Snug pub)
- 7.8 km Oak Bay Marina (café and restaurant)
- 8.9 km Glenlyon-Norfolk School (formerly Francis Rattenbury's home, "Iechineel," built in the early 1900s.)
- 9.3 km Willows Park

④ (10.3km/6.4mi)   Turn R into Cattle Point. (This is part of the 31-hectare/77-acre Uplands Park.)

⑤ (10.9km/6.8mi)   Turn R back onto Beach Drive. (There are numerous beach access points as you pass through this very select neighbourhood called Uplands.)

⑥ (13.0km/8.1mi)   At the crest of a long, gentle hill you'll pass through the Uplands gates, then continue downhill onto Cadboro Bay Road. (At 13.7km/8.5mi is Cadboro Bay Village.) At 14.5km/9.0mi you can detour into Ten Mile Point by turning R onto Tudor Road.

⑦ (14.7km/9.1mi)   Continue past a stop sign onto Telegraph Bay Road.

⑧ (15.1km/9.4mi)   Turn L onto Queenswood Drive, a lumpy but thoroughly secluded road.

⑨ (16.9km/10.5mi)   Turn R onto Arbutus Road.

⑩ (17.8km/11.1mi)   At a stop sign turn R onto a continuation of Arbutus Road.

⑪ (18.9km/11.7mi)   Turn R onto Gordon Head Road. (At 19.3 km Gordon Head Road bears L and becomes Ferndale Road.)

⑫ (19.8km/12.3mi)   Turn R to continue on Ferndale, then bear L onto Tyndall.

⑬ (21.0km/13.0mi)   Turn R onto Ash Road.

⑭	(22.7km/14.1mi)	Turn R onto Cordova Bay Road (aka Mount Douglas Parkway) to ride through the wooded thoroughfare on the eastern edge of Mount Douglas Park. (The entrance to the park's beach and picnic area is at this junction, on your R.)
⑮	(24.6km/15.3mi)	Turn R at the 4-way traffic lights onto a continuation of Cordova Bay Road.
⑯	(28.0km/17.4mi)	Turn R into the carpark of Mattick's Farm shopping area. You'll find a grocery store, café and gift shops galore here. (At this point you can call it a day and arrange to get picked up or you can retrace your route back to Beacon Hill Park [for a total of 56km/35mi] or you can continue with the following described route.)
⑰		From the entrance to Mattick's Farm, cross Cordova Bay Road (with caution) and take Lochside Drive directly opposite. (This is part of the Lochside Trail.)
⑱	(30.8km/19.1mi)	Continue straight on the short paved section of the Lochside Trail. (Maplegrove Road descends to your L.)
⑲	(31.1km/19.3mi)	Continue straight on the continuation of Lochside Drive.
⑳	(31.7km/19.7mi)	Turn L onto Royal Oak Drive.
㉑	(32.3km/20.1mi)	Turn R onto Blenkinsop Road. (The Galey Farm is at 35.5km/22mi. In the summer months, there are also numerous small roadside veggie and flower stalls.)
㉒	(36.0km/22.4mi)	Cross McKenzie Avenue at the traffic lights.

㉓ (36.6km/22.7mi)   Cross Cedar Hill Cross Road at the traffic lights.

㉔ (38.5km/23.9mi)   Turn L at the traffic lights onto Cook Street. You now follow Cook Street back to Dallas Road (Cook Street Village is at 43.0km/26.7mi)

㉕ (43.5km/27mi)   Turn R onto Dallas Road and ride back to your start.

Top: *Harpoon Rock at Harling Point.*
Bottom: *Yes, this is Victoria, British Columbia.*

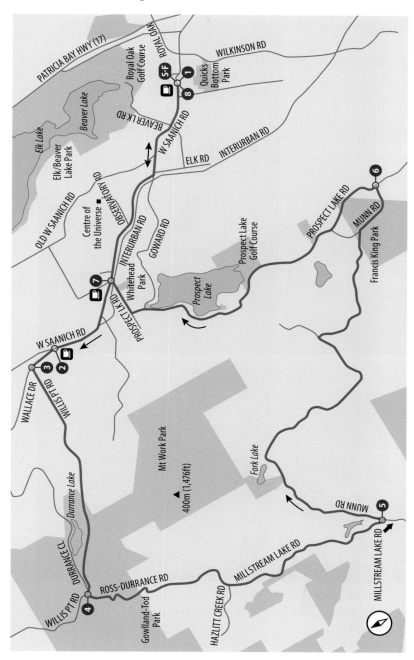

Tour of the Highlands

Despite this tour's start and finish on the southern edge of the Saanich Peninsula, the majority of the time you'll be riding through the rural municipality of Highlands. Aptly named, this is one of the hillier yet scenically pleasing areas of Greater Victoria. Yes, there are patches of farmland, but for the most part the land is wooded. The reason for this is two-fold. First, its residents prefer to keep the forest intact for ecological, aesthetic and privacy reasons. Second, as you might appreciate once you've ridden the route, a large part of the municipality has been, over the years, appropriated as parkland, both by the provincial government and by the Capital Regional District. The largest of the parks is the Gowlland-Tod Provincial Park. Established in 1995, the park comprises well over 1200 hectares and has two distinct habitats. One is the forested upland hills and bluffs and the other is coastal, along the waters of Saanich Inlet and Finlayson Arm. Two other parks – Mt. Work and Francis/King – lie within the municipality and are both spectacular in different ways. Francis/King for its deep coniferous forest and Mt. Work, at 450m/1,476ft, for its splendid views from the peninsula's highest point. All three parks are easily accessible from the route of your ride if you have the time, inclination or energy to explore them.

DISTANCE	36km/22mi.
LEVEL	Strenuous.
HIGHLIGHTS	Little traffic; narrow, hilly roads and deep forested areas; passes or goes through three of the region's most spectacular parks.
START	Take Blanshard Street to the outskirts of the city, where Blanshard becomes the Pat Bay Highway (BC 17). After about 8km/5mi take exit #11, Royal Oak Drive, and turn L. Continue along the highway, and

at the third traffic light turn R onto West Saanich Road. The route begins some 400m/yd along, on the R, from the parking lot adjacent to a small row of stores.

The route

① From the carpark turn R onto West Saanich Road. Pass the entrance to the Centre of the Universe after 3km/2mi on the R. (It's a 1.5km/0.9mi hill climb to the observatory.)

② (5.5km/3.1mi) Turn L onto Wallace Drive just past a farmers market on the L.

③ (6.0km/3.7mi) Turn L again onto Willis Point Road.

④ (10.0km/6.2mi) It's now L onto Ross-Durrance Road, a winding, hilly route that takes you into the heart of the rugged Highlands municipality. Immediately, you pass the entrances to both Mount Work Regional Park R and Gowlland-Tod Provincial Park L. (**Note:** Ross-Durrance becomes Millstream Lake Road at Hazlitt Creek Road, so don't be confused at your next intersection.)

⑤ (16.3km/10.1mi) At the stop sign turn sharply L onto the first hill of Munn Road. This road skirts Mount Work's southern entrance before bisecting Francis/King Regional Park just before its intersection with Prospect Lake Road.

⑥ (25.6km/15.9mi) Turn L onto Prospect Lake Road. At 30km/18.6mi Prospect Lake comes into view on the R. A further 1.5km/0.9 is the small Whitehead

		Park, with beach access and picnic area.
⑦	(32.0km/19.9mi)	Turn R onto West Saanich Road. Across the road are a café and a gas station.
⑧	(36.0km/22.4mi)	Turn L into the carpark where the ride began.

Winter hill climbing.

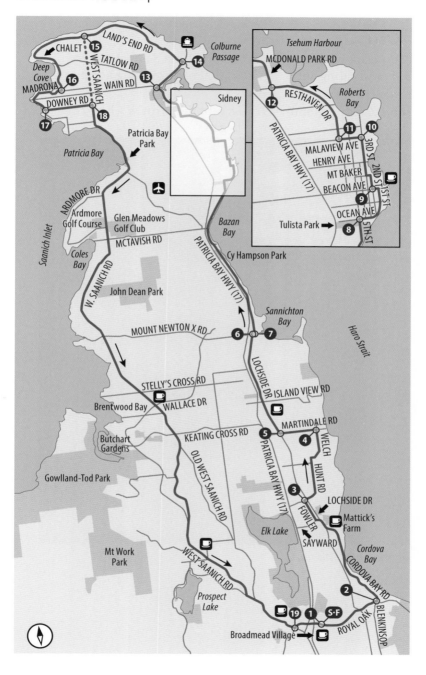

Tour of the Saanich Peninsula

For local riding enthusiasts this route, perhaps more than any other, defines riding enjoyment in the Victoria area. Though there are some hills, the ride takes you closest to local waters for the longest possible time as you will ever get.

Glancing at the ride's map you'll notice right away that you're effectively riding around the perimeter of a large peninsula. On its eastern side you're overlooking Haro Strait, a wide body of water that separates, at this point, the southeastern part of Vancouver Island and the San Juan Islands of the United States. On clear days you can see the volcanic peak of Mt. Baker rising above the San Juan Islands.

On the western shore are the waters of Saanich Inlet, a deep and incisive stretch of water that divides the peninsula from the main island. As you ride this coastline you get views of the wooded slopes of the Malahat summit and, to the north, the community of Mill Bay. You'll also ride into the charming enclave of Deep Cove. Its twisty, shore-hugging lanes and selection of attractive waterfront homes make it one of the highlights of this spectacular ride.

The north end of the peninsula is traversed by the undulations of Lands End Road. Besides getting great views of Salt Spring Island across Satellite Channel you'll ride past some of the most expensive real estate in BC.

Once past the community of Brentwood Bay, you lose the water but you gain rolling pastures and thick roadside forest. Although the city is only a few kilometres/miles away, you'd never know it riding the route back to Broadmead.

DISTANCE	66km/41mi.
LEVEL	Moderate.
HIGHLIGHTS	Coastline views east and west; rural roads; town

of Sidney; Lands End Road and views of Salt Spring Island; Deep Cove; Brentwood Bay.

START From Victoria, take Blanshard Street out of town. Continue on Pat Bay Highway (17) and, after 8km/5mi, take the Royal Oak Drive exit, turning R onto Royal Oak Drive. Some 100 metres/yards along Royal Oak Drive, on the R, is the Broadmead Village Shopping Centre carpark, where the route begins.

The route

① Exit the Broadmead Village Shopping Centre parking lot and turn R onto Royal Oak Drive.

② (2.3km/1.4mi) Turn L at the four-way traffic lights onto Cordova Bay Road. You'll pass Mattick's Farm at 6km/3.7mi. Cordova Bay Road becomes Fowler Road shortly after.

③ (7.2km/4.5mi) Turn R onto Hunt Road. (Sayward Road hill goes to the L.) Hunt becomes Welch Road at 8.8km/5.5mi.

④ (10.2km/6.3mi) Turn L onto Martindale Road.

⑤ (11.5km/7.1mi) Turn R onto Lochside Drive, part of the Lochside Trail. Cross Island View Road at 12.8km/8mi. (The road becomes a smooth asphalt trail shortly after crossing Island View.)

⑥ (15.7km/9.7mi) Turn R onto Mt. Newton Cross Road. (A Quality Inn motel is on the L.)

⑦ (16.0km/9.9mi) Turn L at the stop sign, onto Lochside Drive.

⑧ (22.1km/13.7mi) After passing Tulista Park on your R, turn R onto Ocean Avenue. You'll pass the Anacortes ferry terminal R. Ocean becomes 1st Street at this point, which in turn intersects with

Beacon Avenue. (If you're interested in seeing more of Sidney, this is a good place to start. Beacon Avenue is the town's main thoroughfare.)

⑨ (23.1km/14.3mi)   Turn L onto Beacon Avenue at a small roundabout, then sharp R onto 2nd Street. After a further 200m/yd, at the end of 2nd, turn L onto Mt. Baker Avenue and then R onto 3rd Street. (Sounds complicated but it's not.)

⑩ (24.3km/15.1mi)   Turn L onto Malaview Avenue at the BC Ferries sign.

⑪ (24.7km15.3mi)   Turn R onto Resthaven Drive at the grocery store R.

⑫ (26.5km/16.5km)   Turn R onto McDonald Road at the North Saanich School R.

⑬ (28.0km/17.4mi)   Turn R onto the Pat Bay Highway. Keep to the shoulder and follow signs for Lands End Road. (You can also take Lochside Trail, which parallels the highway, following the signs to Lands End Road.)

⑭ (29.2km/29.2mi)   Once on the off-ramp, move to the L and turn L at the traffic lights, riding over the highway to go straight onto Lands End Road.

⑮ (33.4km20.7mi)   West Saanich Road to your L. (This is a possible alternative route saving about 7km/4.3mi. You'd join the described route at checkpoint 18.) At 35.1km/21.8mi Lands End becomes Chalet Road. At Tatlow Road you'll pass the Deep Cove Chalet restaurant on your R.

⑯ (37.4km/23.2mi)   Turn R onto Birch Road. After

a steep downhill and rise, Birch becomes Madrona Drive. Continue on Madrona past Wain Road.

⑰ (39.1km/24.3mi)   Just before Madrona dead ends, turn L onto Downey Road.

⑱ (40.6km/25.2mi)   Turn R onto West Saanich Road. You'll stay on this road for the next 24km/15mi, so relax and enjoy the scenery. (You do pass some area landmarks on the way, such as Patricia Bay Park; the airport; Brentwood Bay village; and Benvenuto Avenue – the road to Butchart Gardens.)

⑲ (64.8km/40.3mi)   At the top of a steepish hill is the traffic-light junction of West Saanich Road with Wilkinson Road and Royal Oak Drive. Turn L here onto Royal Oak Drive. You soon cross the Pat Bay Highway, after which you turn R into Broadmead Village shopping centre parking lot.

Opposite: *Springtime riding.*
Top: *Lands End Road.*
Bottom: *West Saanich Road, Patricia Bay.*

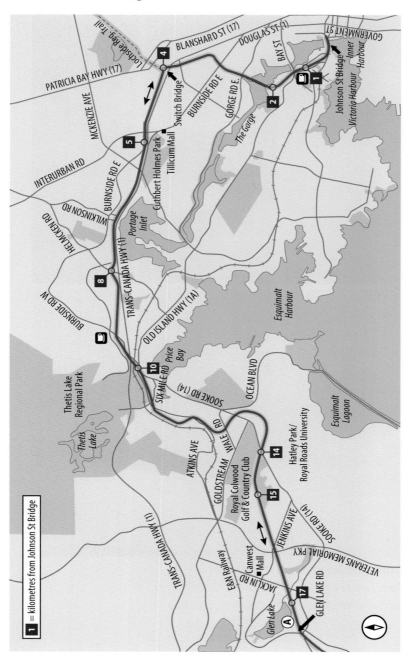

Galloping Goose Regional Trail / Lochside Regional Trail

Shortly after the turn of the twentieth century, Victoria had five working railways that ran out of the city to service Sooke, the Saanich Peninsula, Nanaimo, Port Alberni and Courtenay.

The line for the "Galloping Goose" gas-powered railcar was developed by the Canadian Northern Pacific Railway (which became part of the Canadian National Railways in 1918). It had its first run in 1922 carrying mail and a maximum of 30 passengers from Victoria to Sooke. Although the line continued to Cowichan Lake, the passenger service to Sooke ended in 1931. However, the freight service to Cowichan continued until the 1950s. The Goose's 55km/34mi portion of the line was acquired by the Capital Regional District in 1987 and opened to the public as a trail a year later. Much work has been done on the trail over the years with its first 13km/8mi pavement. Its terminus is what is locally known as Leechtown, an abandoned gold mining operation at the confluence of the Sooke and Leech rivers, and is also part of Kapoor Regional Park.

The Lochside Trail was once one of three railway lines that ran up the Saanich Peninsula. To compete with the British Columbia Railway Company (BCRC) which ran up the west side of the peninsula (started in 1912) and the Victoria and Sidney Railway (V&S) (started in 1894), which ran up the middle, the Canadian Northern Pacific Railway (CNPR) chose, in 1915, to build a line on the peninsula's eastern side. Although all three lines met their demise during the economically depressed 1930s, stretches of each exist today as trails for our use, the CNPR line being the Lochside Trail.

Since both trails are linear and you can't get lost, I've

departed here from the format of the rest of the rides in this book. For those not wanting to ride their whole lengths, here are a few suggestions for rides along particularly interesting sections of these flat trails. Suggested rides are indicated by letters. For those wanting to ride the whole length of the trails, their joint start is on the town side of the Johnson Street Bridge. The Lochside Trail diverges R after 4km/2.5mi, just over the Switch Bridge on the edge of town. The "Goose" is 55km/34mi in length (110km/68mi out and back). The Sooke Potholes Provincial Park's campground is at 51km/31.7mi from town. The Lochside Trail is 33km/20.5mi from town to its terminus at the Swartz Bay ferry terminal. (For the touring cyclist arriving and departing the Island by ferry, it's a great way to get to and from Victoria.) Round trip is 66km/41mi. The seaside town of Sidney is a delightful place to visit on the route.

Trail etiquette: Keep right except to pass; sound your bell or shout "bike" to let others know you're coming; control your speed; be aware of pedestrians, horse riders and other cyclists; respect the environment. (**Note:** trail distance markers are in kilometres.)

THE GALLOPING GOOSE TRAIL

For the adventuresome cyclist, an out-and-back ride along the length of the "Goose" is a rewarding long ride. Because the line was built with no more than a 2 per cent gradient, there are no long hills to trundle up (or speed down). However, there are a few steep pitches where short trestles once spanned gullies and depressions. With good gearing these ups and downs are quite manageable.

(Short out-and-back routes)

A. Starting at the 18 kilometre mark next to the Luxton Fairgrounds, ride to Roche Cove Regional Park. This section offers

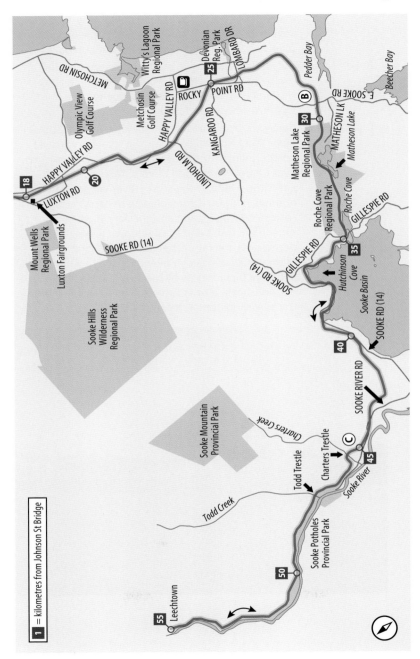

1 = kilometres from Johnson St Bridge

views of the ocean, tree-lined and grassy-verged segments and the chance to visit Matheson Lake for a dip and/or a picnic. (34km/21mi out and back)

B. For a shorter version of the above, start just before the kilometre 30 mark on Rocky Point Road, riding above the shores of Matheson Lake to Roche Cove. (10km/6.2mi out and back)

C. Just before the 44km/27mi point at the parking area off Sooke River Road (the trail crosses the road here) travel north, riding over the two sweeping trestle bridges over Charters and Todd creeks. This section to Leechtown follows the Sooke River very closely at times and you'll get a chance to pause at the restored Barnes Station on the way in. As you approach the trail's end at Leechtown (a long-abandoned gold-mining settlement at the confluence of the Sooke and Leech rivers) there are a number of choice picnic spots by the river. (22km/13.5mi out-and-back) (For information on B&Bs close to the Goose visit gallopinggoosetrail.com).

Opposite: *The Selkirk Trestle.*
Top: *Sooke Basin from Roche Cove.*
Bottom: *Sooke Basin from the Galloping Goose Trail.*

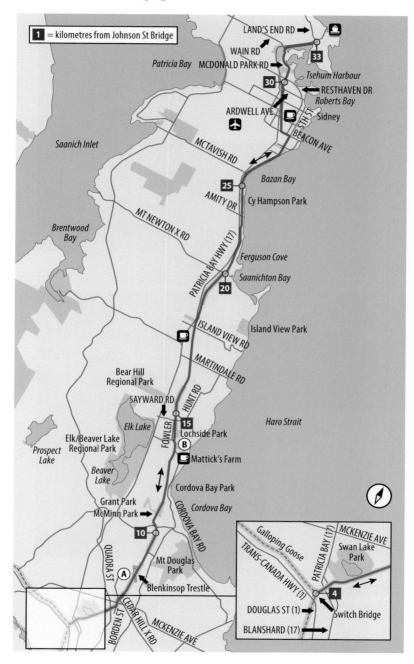

1 = kilometres from Johnson St Bridge

LAND'S END RD →

WAIN RD

Patricia Bay   MCDONALD PARK RD

33

Tsehum Harbour

30

RESTHAVEN DR
Roberts Bay

ARDWELL AVE

Sidney

Saanich Inlet

MCTAVISH RD

BEACON AVE

5TH ST

Bazan Bay

25

AMITY DR   Cy Hampson Park

MT NEWTON X RD

Brentwood
Bay

PATRICIA BAY HWY (17)

Ferguson Cove

20   Saanichton Bay

ISLAND VIEW RD

Island View Park

Bear Hill
Regional Park

MARTINDALE RD

HUNT RD

SAYWARD RD

Haro Strait

Elk Lake

15

FOWLER

Lochside Park

B

Elk/Beaver Lake
Regional Park

Mattick's Farm

Prospect
Lake

Beaver
Lake

Cordova Bay Park

Grant Park

Cordova Bay

McMinn Park →

CORDOVA BAY RD

10

QUADRA ST

Mt Douglas
Park

A

Blenkinsop Trestle

CEDAR HILL X RD

BORDEN ST

MCKENZIE AVE

Galloping Goose

MCKENZIE AVE

PATRICIA BAY (17)

Swan Lake
Park

TRANS-CANADA HWY (1)

4

DOUGLAS ST (1) →

Switch Bridge

BLANSHARD (17) →

From its start at the Johnson Street Bridge, this trail travels 33 kilometres all the way to the Swartz Bay ferry terminal. At 30 km it crosses Beacon Avenue in Sidney. There are a number of cafes in this lovely seaside town, which makes it a perfect destination for an out-and-back ride from Victoria. (Over the years, this has become a quasi-ritualistic morning ride for many local cyclists.)

(Short out-and-back routes)

A. From the trail's parking area on Lochside Drive just north of McKenzie Avenue, ride over the 288m/315yd-long Blenkinsop Trestle and then along the side of Cordova Ridge on Lochside Drive to finish at Mattick's Farm for tea or coffee. (15km/9.3mi out and back)

B. Begin at Lochside Park. From there ride along the avenue of trees and then into the open farmland paralleling the Pat Bay Highway. Continue along Lochside Drive, passing Cy Hampson Park at about the 25-kilometre marker, and then on to the oceanside Tulista Park, which marks the entrance to the town of Sidney. If you want to explore the town, ride the extra 1km/0.6mi to the town's main street, Beacon Avenue. (26km/16mi out and back)

Lochside Trail.

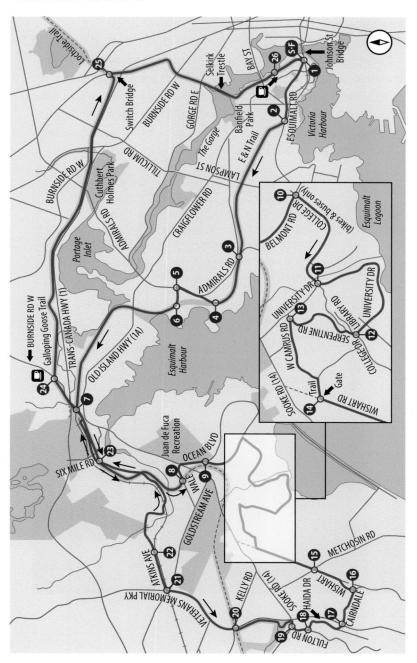

E&N Trail / Royal Roads U. / Galloping Goose Regional Trail

Royal Roads University, a relatively young creation, rose out of the proverbial ashes of a military college which had occupied the extensive and beautiful grounds of Hatley Park since 1940. The park is dominated by the crenellated tower of Hatley Castle, which James Dunsmuir, a coal and railway baron, had built in 1909. The wealthy Scot commissioned the well-known Victoria architect Samuel Maclure to design what he hoped would be his family's ancestral home. Two Boston landscape artists planned the grounds and gardens.

Dunsmuir's hoped-for dynasty never transpired, and in 1940 the federal government bought the 228-hectare estate for $75,000. The present-day campus encompasses a variety of habitats, including dense forest, open parkland, a lagoon, a lake, formal gardens and a creek complete with gorge and waterfalls. Frankly, there's nowhere in Victoria's vicinity where so much variety exists.

Entrepreneurial verve and pioneering vision of both national and local railway builders are responsible for the two regional trails you'll ride on in following the route described below.

Incredibly, at the turn of the twentieth century, there were five working railway lines that ran from Victoria to service Sooke, Nanaimo, Port Alberni, Courtenay and the Saanich Peninsula. The longest of the bunch is the Esquimalt & Nanaimo (E&N) line, which, while not operational since 2011, ran passenger and freight service between Victoria and Courtenay, a town 235 kilometres/146 miles to the north. It started operations in 1883 and eventually reached Courtenay in 1914.

Construction of the E&N trail, which parallels the eponymous rail line, began in 2009. The route is now paved and stretches almost 9 kilometres/5.6miles from Victoria to View Royal. While not totally scenic, the trail gives you a glimpse of suburban Victoria.

The "Galloping Goose" was a gas-powered railcar developed by the Canadian Northern Pacific Railway (later part of the Canadian National Railway). It ran from 1922, carrying mail and passengers from Victoria to Sooke. Although the line continued to Lake Cowichan, the passenger service to Sooke ended in 1931. Freight to Lake Cowichan ran until the early 1950s. The Capital Regional District acquired the Goose's 55km/34mi portion of the line in 1987 and opened it to the public as a linear park and trail a year later. You'll be riding on part of the trail's smooth, paved surface. (**Note:** You'll also read a variation of these last three paragraphs in the introduction to the Galloping Goose and Lochside Trail routes.)

DISTANCE	35km/22mi.
LEVEL	Easy to moderate.
HIGHLIGHTS	Two locally significant railway-associated trails; Royal Roads University's Hatley Park and castle; views over Esquimalt Lagoon to the Olympic Mountains; the Selkirk Trestle over Victoria's Upper Harbour.

The route

① From the downtown side of the Johnson Street Bridge, ride across the bridge and continue straight on Esquimalt Road.

② (1.3km/0.8mi) After the traffic lights at Catherine Street take the R-turning bike lane at Springfield Street onto the E&N trail. You're now essentially following the train tracks to View Royal.

③ (3.9km/2.4mi)   Having crossed six intersections, you now arrive at a complicated four-way crossing. Make for the trail at the far R corner. Obeying traffic rules and your common sense, cross Admirals Road keeping to the sidewalk rather than the green bike path. This will allow an easier re-entry to the trail.

④ (5.4km/3.3mi)   The trail rises slightly to parallel Admirals Road.

⑤ (5.8km/3.6mi)   At Hallowell Road the trail turns L.

⑥ (6.1km/3.8mi)   Crossing R near the end of Hallowell, take the trail as it resumes paralleling the E&N rail tracks.

⑦ (8.9km/5.5mi)   After dropping down to street level, the trail crosses the busy four-lane intersection at a light-controlled crosswalk to join the Galloping Goose Regional Trail. At the Goose, turn L onto the trail.

⑧ (11.6km/7.2mi)   As the trail intersects Wale Road, cross Wale via the crosswalk and turn L, riding in Wale's bike lane. You're now leaving the trail. After 200m/yd, cross the Old Island Highway onto Ocean Boulevard.

⑨ (12.2km/7.6mi)   Ocean Boulevard forks L, while you continue straight onto Belmont Road. You are now entering Belmont Park, a housing complex for the Canadian Forces.

⑩ (12.9km/8.0mi)   Turn R onto College Road. You'll recognize the turn by the distinctive stone and mock Tudor building on the road's R corner. After 400m/yd pass through the gates into Royal Roads University, where College Road becomes College Drive. (On weekends, the road gates are locked, so you have to enter by the adjacent pedestrian gate.)

⑪ (14.0km/8.7mi)   At College Drive's end, turn L onto University Drive. The entrance to historic Hatley Castle is directly opposite. Descend on University Drive as it swings R to brush the shore of Esquimalt Lagoon. The road soon bears R to gently climb back up to some of the university buildings.

⑫ (15.3km/9.5mi)   At a stop sign, turn R onto College Drive. Library Road goes immediately R. You bear L to stay on College Drive. After a short, steep pitch, and as College goes straight, you turn sharply L to continue climbing on the one-way Serpentine Road. While not exactly serpentine, the road does have its twists. And it is steep.

⑬ (16.1km/10mi)   Serpentine ends at West Campus Road. Turn L here onto West Campus. Keep to West Campus for a short while (about 600m/yd) and, just as the road turns L, look for and take a gravel path beside a double-wide gate on your R. This a brief path which ends at a gate that exits onto Wishart Road.

⑭ (17.6km/10.9mi)   Pass through the gate and turn L onto Wishart.

⑮ (18.6km/11.5mi)   Cross over Metchosin Road at the traffic lights to continue on Wishart.

⑯	(19.5km/12.1mi)	Pass Wishart Elementary School on your R and then, two blocks later, turn R onto Cairndale Road.
⑰	(20.2km/12.5mi)	Cross Veterans Memorial Parkway to continue on Cairndale for a very short distance, then turn R at the stop sign onto Haida Drive.
⑱	(20.9km/13.0mi)	As Haida Drive intersects Fulton Road you turn R onto Fulton and ride down to its junction with Sooke Road aka Highway 14.
⑲	(21.0km/13.1mi)	Turn R onto Sooke Road and immediately move into the L turning lane. Turn L onto the crosswalk to find and follow a descending trail. Keep to this trail as it meanders close to Veterans Memorial Parkway.
⑳	(22.1km/13.7mi)	The trail ends at the junction of Kelly Road and Veterans Memorial Parkway. Cross Kelly on the crosswalk and then head R across Veterans. Turn L to ride north on the wide shoulder of Veterans.
㉑	(23.4km/14.5mi)	Keeping to the bike lane, you ignore the R exit lane at the second set of lights at the next junction and cross Goldstream Avenue, the main road coming from the R. Take care traversing the rail tracks and then turn R onto the sidewalk on the far side of Goldstream. Follow the sidewalk past the Langford welcome sign and insignia to Atkins Avenue. Ride on Atkins's bike lane.
㉒	(24.7km/15.3mi)	Turn R at a four-way stop sign onto the continuation of Atkins.

㉓ (26.7km/16.6mi)   As Atkins bears L turn R onto the signed Galloping Goose Regional Trail. A trail "pit stop" is a couple of hundred metres/yards along this stretch of trail.

㉔ (27.7km/17.2mi)   The trail turns abruptly R to cross Burnside Road West. You now stay on the trail until it junctions with the Lochside Trail.

㉕ (33.2km/20.6mi)   As the trail veers L to become the Lochside Trail, you bear R to stay on the Goose and cross the Switch Bridge. There follows a number of marked intersections at all of which you have the right of way. The highlight of this section of the Goose

is the 300m/yd-long Selkirk Trestle, a well preserved vestige of Victoria's almost century-old fascination with railways.

㉖ (33.7km/20.9mi) You turn sharp R as the trail meets Harbour Road. Although the road doesn't look like a trail, its bike lane is an official part of the Goose. At Harbour Road's junction with Esquimalt Road, turn L to finish the ride by pedalling over the Johnson Street Bridge.

Opposite: *An E&N station.*
Top: *Esquimalt and Mt. Olympus.*
Bottom: *Hatley Castle.*

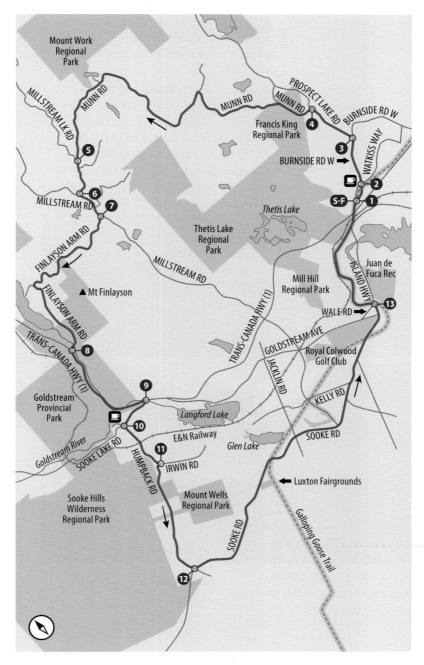

Highlands / Humpback / Galloping Goose Loop

This 38 kilometre/23.5 mile ride is never very far from the country's iconic vehicular artery, the Trans-Canada Highway. In fact, it starts a stone's throw from one of its local intersections, the Colwood exit. But don't be discouraged. The route described here draws a large circle around the highway and takes you into the hills on both its flanks. For the most part you'll never know it's there.

Like the other rides in this book that go into the Highlands and Langford areas this one has its fair share of ups and downs. The one "down" that is spectacular is the descent off Millstream Road along Finlayson Arm Road and into Goldstream Provincial Park. The west side of Mt. Finlayson rises precipitously above your left shoulder while the marshy waters of the butt-end of Finlayson Arm lay below to your right as you follow the narrow, twisting road through the tall conifers on its way to Goldstream Park.

Once across the Trans-Canada you enter the eastern edge of the Sooke Hills. This large forested area is a wilderness preserve, and Humpback Road squeezes between two of the preserve's smaller peaks – Mount McDonald and Mount Wells. You'll see information signs along the road indicating the hiking trails that ribbon these hills.

The final short stretch of the ride is along the Galloping Goose Trail, allowing you to relax a little as you trundle along this traffic-free grade. (**Note:** The Galloping Goose Trail is gravel from the Luxton Fairgrounds to its junction with Ocean Boulevard and Wale Road.)

DISTANCE	38km/24mi.

LEVEL	Moderate to strenuous.
HIGHLIGHTS	A ride through one of the region's hilliest and most forested areas; proximity to four of the areas parks; ride down on of the area's steepest descents; great scenery; great exercise.
START	The Galloping Goose Trail's Atkins Road trailhead carpark in View Royal, west of Victoria.

HOW TO GET THERE

Driving:	From downtown follow Douglas Street/Trans-Canada Highway out of town for 10km/6mi. On your R, take the Colwood exit, #10. Almost immediately after, the three underpasses turn R into the signed Galloping Goose Trail's Atkins Road carpark.
Cycling:	From the Johnson Street Bridge take the Galloping Goose Regional Trail to just before the 10 kilometre marker at the Atkins Road trailhead (where there are toilets, a water fountain and shelter) and turn L at the traffic light onto Burnside Road West at check-point 2 below.

The route

①		From the Galloping Goose Trail's Atkins Road carpark turn R onto the trail going east (toward Victoria).
②	(1.1km/0.7mi)	Turn L at the traffic lights onto Burnside Road West. (The trail continues across the road.)
③	(2.3km/1.4mi)	Turn L onto Prospect Lake Road.
④	(3.5km/2.2mi)	Turn L onto Munn Road. A short distance on the R is the entrance to Francis/King Regional Park. (At 11km/6.8mi is the trailhead to Mt. Work Regional Park on R.)
⑤	(12.9km/8.0mi)	At the bottom of a steep hill, turn L

at the stop sign onto Millstream Lake Road.

(6) (13.9km/8.6mi) At the stop sign turn L onto Millstream Road. (Don't be confused by the similar-sounding names.)

(7) (14.7km/9.1mi) Turn R onto Finlayson Arm Road. (This road is a mostly narrow and very steep downhill. Take care!)

(8) (19.9km/12.4mi) You're now at the junction with the Trans-Canada Highway and this is also an entrance to Goldstream Provincial Park. (You've just passed the trailhead to the 419-metre (1,375-ft) Mount Finlayson on your L.) Turn L onto the highway. (Be careful of the traffic. There is a reasonably wide shoulder, and bear in mind you're only on it for 2.5 km/1.5mi.)

(9) (22.4km/13.9mi) Watch for a row of concrete barriers R and turn R through these barriers onto the dead end of Sooke Lake Road. Turn L and then R again at the road's junction with Amy Road and Canyon Park Place to continue on Sooke Lake Road.

(10) (23.2km/14.4mi) At Ma Miller's Pub turn L onto Humpback Road. Sometimes there are road barriers to be negotiated halfway up the hill.

(11) (24.5km/15.2mi) Take the R fork at Humpback and Irwin Road to continue on Humpback Road. A carpark for Mount Wells Regional Park and the Sooke Hills Wilderness Regional Park is just past this fork on the R. Humpback is a

narrow road with restricted visibility in parts. Take care! Again.

⑫ (27.6km/17.1mi) Turn L onto Sooke Road.

⑬ (36.4km/22.6mi) At the major intersection of Wale Road, Ocean Boulevard and Sooke Road (aka Old Island Highway), turn L onto Wale Road. After 200m/yd turn R onto the paved Galloping Goose at Wilfert Road to begin the 2km/1.2mi back to the Atkins Road carpark and the ride's start.

Opposite: *Humpback Road.*
Above: *A possible detour?*

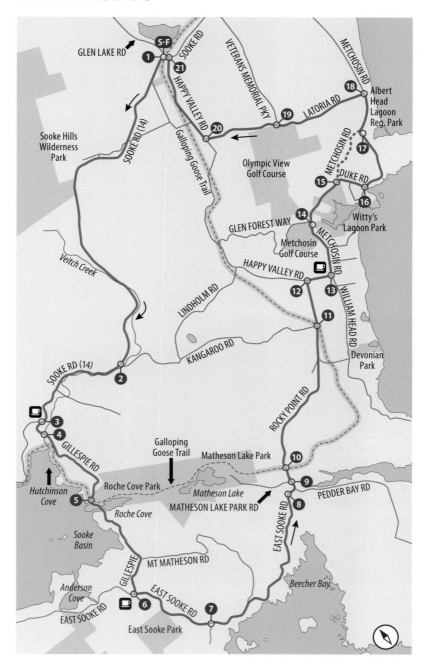

Metchosin / East Sooke Loop

Despite the hilly nature of this route, it's a great ride and you'll get to see, close up, a number of the area's special places.

You'll start off rather calmly on the main road to Sooke, but after the 17 Mile Pub, you venture into the hills. Your first plunge takes you down to sea level at Roche Cove. This lovely inlet is at the western end of two connected regional parks – Roche Cove Park and Matheson Lake Park. From the cove there are wonderful views of Sooke Basin, and the surrounding hills hold some of the area's oldest cedars.

As you ride along East Sooke Road you'll pass Becher Bay Road and then the Aylard Farm entrance to the magnificent East Sooke Park. A visit here will not disappoint no matter what the season. The park is often described as a mystical place where the forest meets the sea and is regarded as the place where the West Coast truly begins. It's the largest of the regional parks and covers almost 1500 hectares/3,700 acres. The Aylard Farm trailhead offers a picnic site and a small sandy beach. Not far past Becher Bay Road, Becher Bay will come into view on the right. Dotted with small islands, the bay focuses the eye on the waters of the Strait of Juan de Fuca and the Olympic Mountains beyond.

The entrance to two other parks – Matheson Lake and Witty's Lagoon – are along this road. Both are worth a visit if time permits. If the hills become too much or time becomes limited there is always the Galloping Goose Trail as an escape route. You're never far from this trail and you cross it three times on this ride.

DISTANCE	43km/27mi.
LEVEL	Moderate to strenuous.
HIGHLIGHTS	The regional parks of Roche Cove, East Sooke,

	Matheson Lake and Witty's Lagoon; ocean and mountain views; Metchosin village and church.
START	The Galloping Goose Trail's Page Avenue parking area in Langford.

HOW TO GET THERE

Driving:	Take Douglas Street/Trans-Canada Highway out of town. After 10km/6.2mi take the Colwood exit R onto the Old Island Highway (14). Follow the highway (which becomes Sooke Road) for about 6km/3.7mi until, at a sharp L bend just past the Happy Valley Road junction, you turn R onto Glen Lake Road and then immediately R again onto Page Avenue. The parking area for the Galloping Goose Trail is just on your R.
Cycling:	Take the Galloping Goose Regional Trail from its trailhead at the Johnson Street Bridge. At the Switch Bridge (4km/2.5mi) turn L to follow the trail in the Sooke direction. Just after the 17 kilometre marker and at the trail's intersection with Glen Lake Road and Sooke Road is the ride's start. Add another 34km/21mi (out-and-back) to your ride.

The route

① From the parking area turn briefly L onto Glen Lake Road and then R onto Sooke Road (Highway 14). Luxton fairground can be seen on your L.

② (9.0km/5.5mi) Pass Kangaroo Road junction on the L.

③ (11.5km/7.1mi) 17 Mile Pub is on your R. (After November 2022 this will be different, as a bypass will take the road behind the pub. However, there will be signs for Gillespie Road, your next turn.)

④ (11.7km/7.3mi)   Just after the pub turn L onto Gillespie Road. (See note above.)

⑤ (14.5km/9.0mi)   Entrance to Roche Cove Regional Park is on the L. The Galloping Goose Trail crosses the road at this point.

⑥ (17.6km/10.9mi)   Turn L onto East Sooke Road.

⑦ (19.6km/12.2mi)   Becher Bay Road runs off to the R. The Aylard Farm entrance to East Sooke Regional Park is at the end of this road, 1.5km/1mi away.

⑧ (24.5km/15.2mi)   At the stop sign turn L onto Rocky Point Road.

⑨ (24.6km/15.3mi)   Matheson Lake Road is on the L. This leads to the entrance to Matheson Lake Regional Park, just over 1.0km/0.6mi away.

⑩ (25.0km/15.5mi)   The Galloping Goose Trail crosses Rocky Point Road.

⑪ (28.7km/17.8mi)   Kangaroo Road junction on L. Also, the Galloping Goose Trail crosses the roadway again.

⑫ (29.8km/18.5mi)   Turn R onto Happy Valley Road.

⑬ (30.4km/18.9mi)   Metchosin village centre where there is a store and café. Turn L at the stop sign onto Metchosin Road. (The old St. Mary the Virgin church is on the L.)

⑭ (31.6km/19.6mi)   Entrance to Witty's Lagoon Regional Park on the R.

⑮ (33.0km/20.5mi)   Turn R onto Duke Road (West). (If you prefer not to take this short but pleasant detour, continue on Metchosin Road to Highway 17. You'll save yourself 1.5km/1mi.)

⑯ (33.6km/20.9mi)	Turn L at the stop sign onto the continuation of Duke Road.
⑰ (35.4km/22.0mi)	Turn R onto Metchosin Road.
⑱ (36.4km/22.6mi)	Turn L onto Latoria Road.
⑲ (38.1km/23.7mi)	Continue on Latoria Road past this signed junction with Veterans Memorial Parkway.
⑳ (40.2km/25.0mi)	Turn R onto Happy Valley Road.
㉑ (42.4km/25.1mi)	At the traffic light you can either turn L onto Sooke Road, then immediately R onto Glen Lake Road and then R to the Page Avenue parking area of the Galloping Goose Trail, or you cross Sooke Road at the crossing and take the short gravel trail to the Goose and turn L. The parking area is on your R.

Opposite: *Winter riding in Metchosin.*
Top: *East Sooke Road.*
Bottom: *Riding in Metchosin.*

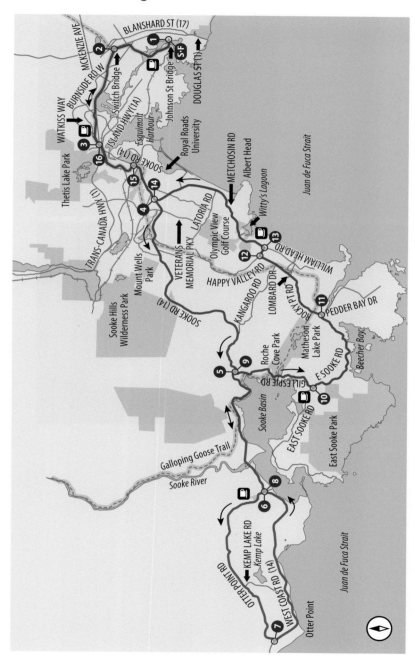

Sooke / Otter Point Loop

Though not an easy ride, this long excursion explores some of the dramatic shorelines, with their attendant ups and downs, that lie west of Victoria along the Strait of Juan de Fuca and the Sooke Basin.

The road out to Sooke is deceptive. Not bad for a country road you might think. A bit twisty, perhaps, but no real hills. But once you get past Sooke onto Otter Point Road and then, on the way back, riding along Gillespie Road into East Sooke and Metchosin, the terrain changes – abruptly.

Before you get to the hills, though, you'll pass a couple of historically interesting sites. As you leave Colwood, about 14km/9mi into the ride, you'll notice, on your L, the entrance to Royal Roads University and Hatley Castle and Park. The castle and land once belonged to the late nineteenth and early twentieth century coal and railway baron James Dunsmuir. Built in 1909, the castle was designed by the well-known Victoria architect Samuel Maclure. Dunsmuir hoped the castle would be the ancestral home of a dynasty of which his father Sir Robert Dunsmuir was the progenitor. It never happened, and in 1940 the federal government purchased the 228-hectare/563-acre estate for $75,000. The park is open to the public and includes a variety of habitat including forest, a lagoon and a creek as well as formal gardens.

Sooke Road's 17 Mile Pub is one of three pubs and restaurants that sprang up along the way between Sooke and Victoria in the mid- to late 1800s. The other two are the 4 Mile Brewpub and Restaurant in View Royal on the Old Island Highway and the Six Mile Pub, also on the Old Island Highway, in Colwood (you pass it not long after leaving the Galloping Goose Trail). These old "coachhouses" served to provide sustenance to early Sooke and Metchosin settlers travelling to and from Victoria.

But, back to the hills. Otter Point Road traces a large arc from the centre of Sooke to the waters of the Strait of Juan de Fuca. It's only about 11km/7mi long but its hilly, twisty contours give a roller-coaster of a ride. Turning onto Gillespie Road at almost 70km/43.5mi into the ride you get the thrill of a steep descent to a bridge followed by the grunt of an uphill as the road travels toward Roche Cove. There are other ups and downs before the cove (which is also a regional park and worth a stop), and as the route hits East Sooke Road and Rocky Point Road it gets no flatter. You have to wait until the 96km/60mi mark (where you're back on Sooke Road) before you can relax on a level road and an even quieter paved trail.

DISTANCE	111km/67mi.
LEVEL	Strenuous.
HIGHLIGHTS	Hatley Park; 6 Mile and 17 Mile Pubs; regional parks; challenging and scenic country roads; views over ocean and mountains.
START	Galloping Goose Regional Trail's trailhead at the Johnson Street Bridge in downtown Victoria.

The route

①		From the Galloping Goose Regional Trail's head at the Johnson Street Bridge follow the trail to its intersection with the Trans-Canada Highway.
②	(4.0km/2.4mi)	After crossing the Trans-Canada over the pedestrian/cyclist overpass (aka the Switch Bridge) turn L, following the Galloping Goose Trail as it runs parallel to the highway.
③	(9.5km/6.0mi)	At the trail's traffic-light intersection

with West Burnside Road and Watkiss Way, turn L onto the roadway of West Burnside, riding under the highway to join the Old Island Highway as it runs through the suburb of Colwood. After the junction with Goldstream Avenue the road becomes Sooke Road (Highway 14). Look for Royal Roads University and Hatley castle and park, on your L.

④ (14.5km/9.0mi)   Pass the junction with Metchosin Road on your L. (You'll come back along that road many kilometres/ miles later.)

⑤ (30.0km/18.6mi)   Just past the 17 Mile Pub on your R is the intersection with Gillespie Road L, another stretch of pavement you'll become familiar with on your way back. (Sooke Road is scheduled to bypass the pub as of 2022. This might affect the route's course on the way back. Be aware.)

⑥ (38.3km/23.8mi)   In Sooke's town centre, turn R just past a roundabout at the traffic lights onto Otter Point Road.

⑦ (49.6km/30.8mi)   After a longish "roly-poly" ride, at the top of a steep hill, you'll see the ocean and the Olympic Mountains beyond come into view. You soon turn L onto West Coast Road (Highway 14). You're now on your return journey.

⑧ (61.4km/38.2mi)   Continue through the centre of Sooke. (Otter Point Road is off to your L.)

⑨ (69.6km/42.2mi)   Turn R onto Gillespie Road. (The road

		is signed just before the turn, but see note at checkpoint 5.)
⑩	(75.3km/46.8mi)	At the junction with East Sooke Road turn L.
⑪	(82.1km/51.0mi)	A stop sign signals the end of East Sooke Road. Pedder Bay Road goes R; you turn L onto Rocky Point Road.
⑫	(87.5km/54.4mi)	Turn R at the next junction, onto Happy Valley Road.
⑬	(88.1km/54.7mi)	After 600m/yd turn L onto Metchosin Road. (The village centre is here.)
⑭	(96.5km/60.0mi)	Turn R onto Sooke Road, direction Victoria.
⑮	(99.1km/61.6mi)	At the next major junction (Wale Road/Ocean Boulevard) turn L onto Wale, then L onto the paved Galloping Goose Trail 200m/yd farther.
⑯	(102.0km/63.4mi)	Pass the Atkins Road trail rest area. You now follow the Goose back to its start over the Johnson Street Bridge.

Roadside pub.

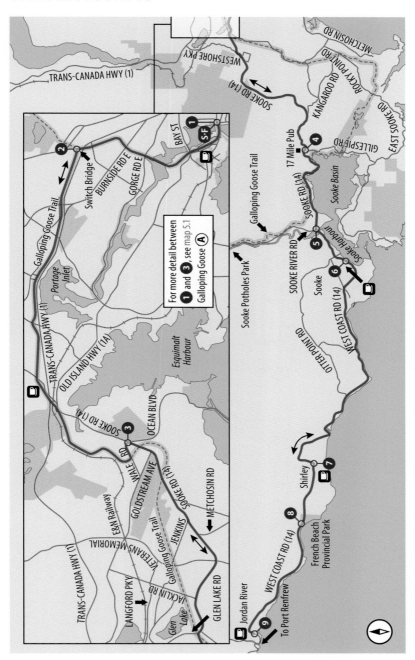

Victoria to Jordan River

For anyone wanting to try their hand at a century ride (usually understood to mean 100 miles, or 160 kilometres), this route out to Jordan River would fit the bill. Though it is 14km/8.7mi short of a "century," you can easily add distance once back in town (an out-and-back along the waterfront, for example). Mind you, the challenging terrain itself will make it feel like you've pedalled a century. Many of the local riding clubs use this destination as a staple of their year-round training regime.

Sooke Road has been much maligned over the years (mainly by fast motorists) for its many bends and narrower sections. Personally, I find it just fine and enjoy its twistiness, lumpiness and its rural flavour. And, it's a great ride to test your fitness while seeing the "rugged" West Coast.

Jordan River itself is a waif of a community. Once a hub of logging activity and hydroelectric generation, it's now better known as a surfing destination with a scenic campground. Originally named by Spanish explorers in the early 1790s as Rio Hermoso, it was then quickly renamed after lead explorer Francisco de Eliza's chaplain, Alejandro Jordan, to Rio Jordan. It's officially named River Jordan, but the not so subtle biblical reference is now lost with its more popular usage as Jordan River.

DISTANCE	146km/90.8mi.
LEVEL	Moderate to strenuous.
HIGHLIGHTS	Hilly terrain; views over the Strait of Juan de Fuca and the Olympic Mountains; delightful coffee stops in Shirley and Jordan River; Sheringham Point lighthouse; beach accesses.
START	Trailhead of the Galloping Goose Regional Trail at the Johnson Street Bridge in downtown Victoria.

The route

①   Leave Victoria on the Galloping Goose Regional Trail at the Johnson Street Bridge.

② (4.0km/2.5mi)   Turn L on the continuation of the "Goose" after the Switch Bridge over the Trans-Canada Highway. Follow this paved trail for 15 kilometres/9.3 miles.

③ (15km/9.3mi)   As the trail intersects the wide Wale Road turn L onto the roadway, ride the 100 metres/yards to the traffic lights and turn R onto Sooke Road (aka Highway 14).

④ (31km/19.2mi)   Pass the 17 Mile House pub on your R. (As of 2022 a realignment of this stretch of Sooke Road was under construction, so this checkpoint might change.)

⑤ (38km/23.6mi)   Cross the Sooke River bridge. The road to your R just before the bridge is the access to Sooke Potholes Provincial Park.

⑥ (40km/25mi)   Continue past the roundabout in Sooke, a community of around 13,000 people. Sooke Road/Highway 14 is now also known as West Coast Road. (About 2.0km/1.2mi past the roundabout you pass Whiffin Spit Road on your L. This leads to a local landmark, Whiffin Spit, a long sandbar jutting into Sooke Harbour.

⑦ (59km/36.5mi)   At the top of a steep hill is the small village of Shirley. On the L is Sheringham Point Road, which leads to the Sheringham Point lighthouse.

A café on the R corner of the highway and Sheringham Point Road is called "Shirley Delicious."

(8) (62km/38.5mi)   Entrance to French Beach Provincial Park on your L.

(9) (73km/45.4mi)   Jordan River. This is your turnaround point. Just across the river and as the road turns north (R), there's the tongue-in-cheek-named "Cold Shoulder Café" if you need to replenish before the return journey.

Relaxing at Jordan River.

VICTORIA ROUTE 11

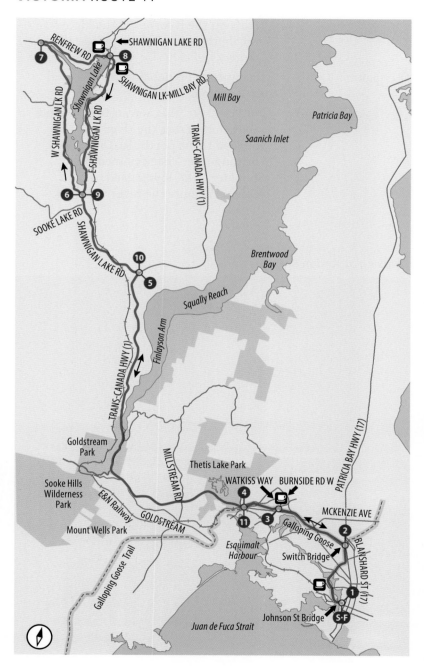

RENFREW RD

SHAWNIGAN LAKE RD

7

8

SHAWNIGAN LK-MILL BAY RD

Shawnigan Lake

W SHAWNIGAN LK RD

E-SHAWNIGAN LK RD

Mill Bay

Patricia Bay

Saanich Inlet

TRANS-CANADA HWY (1)

6 9

SOOKE LAKE RD

SHAWNIGAN LAKE RD

Brentwood Bay

10

5

Squally Reach

Finlayson Arm

TRANS-CANADA HWY (1)

PATRICIA BAY HWY (17)

Goldstream Park

MILLSTREAM RD

Thetis Lake Park

WATKISS WAY   BURNSIDE RD W

Sooke Hills Wilderness Park

E&N Railway

GOLDSTREAM

4

MCKENZIE AVE

Mount Wells Park

11   3

Galloping Goose

2

GOLDSTREAM

Galloping Goose Trail

Esquimalt Harbour

Switch Bridge

BLANSHARD ST (17)

1

Johnson St Bridge

S·F

Juan de Fuca Strait

Victoria / Shawnigan Lake via The Malahat

Not quite a hundred kilometres, or sixty miles, in length, this ride is often regarded by local cyclists and triathletes as the proving ground on which to gauge their fitness and race preparedness.

The ride's beginning on the Galloping Goose Regional Trail at the Johnson Street Bridge is a quick and safe way to leave town, being paved all the way to its intersection with the Trans-Canada Highway.

The two defining sections of this long ride are the Malahat Drive and the ride out of Shawnigan Lake up the 6km/4mi Shawnigan Lake Road hill to the Malahat. The Malahat Drive portion of the Trans-Canada Highway you ride is about 10km/6mi. Both the above hills are quite relentless but both have portions that are flattish, meaning you can catch your breath.

Although you don't necessarily ride the whole length of the Malahat (its summit of 356m/1168ft is only a few kilometres/miles past the Shawnigan Lake south turnoff), its history is interesting. Named after the local Indigenous people, the Malahat, and notwithstanding that a trail of some kind has existed over this protrusive piece of land for millennia, the first thoroughfare of any width was a cattle trail that was cut in 1861. As commerce became more important between the Cowichan Valley and the fledgling community of Victoria, the trail evolved by 1884 into a wagon track. The road was finally paved in 1911. Over the past century the route has gone through many improvements and upgrades. It is a beautiful stretch of road, especially if one looks east. There you see over the Saanich Inlet to the Saanich Peninsula. with the radar towers atop Mount Newton boldly dominating its north end. Beyond are the Gulf Islands and beyond those, Mt. Baker. Another peak, Mt. Finlayson, looms large on the skyline as you descend through Goldstream Provincial Park on the journey back.

DISTANCE	92km/57mi.
LEVEL	Strenuous.
HIGHLIGHTS	The Malahat Drive; views east over the Saanich Peninsula and beyond; the 22km/13.6mi ride around Shawnigan Lake; Shawnigan Lake village.
START	Downtown Victoria at the trailhead of the Galloping Goose Regional Trail at the Johnson Street Bridge.

The route

①		From Galloping Goose Regional Trail trailhead at the Johnson Street Bridge ride to the Switch Bridge that traverses the Trans-Canada Highway.
②	(4.0km/2.5mi)	Just over the bridge, and at a fork, follow the Galloping Goose going L. Over the next few kilometres/miles you'll cross two major intersections: Tillicum Road by a crosswalk and McKenzie Avenue by way of an overpass.
③	(9.0km/5.6mi)	At the trail's traffic-light intersection with West Burnside Road, cross over, keeping to the trail, and ride for a little over 0.5km/300yd before taking a short paved trail on the R to Watkiss Way (this is almost beneath the overpass) and turn L onto Watkiss.
④	(10.0km/6.2mi)	As Watkiss bears R, and behind a bus shelter, take a short and narrow

trail up to the shoulder of the Trans-Canada Highway. Next come two major intersections: exit #14 (Langford, Sooke and Highlands) and exit #16 (Leigh Road).

⑤ (19.7km/12.2mi)   Pass the entrance to Goldstream Provincial Park, which marks the beginning of the Malahat Drive.

⑤ (29.5km/18.3mi)   Roughly 2km/1.2mi after a gas station and restaurant on your R, turn L onto the well-signed Shawnigan Lake Road. (Take care moving into the L-hand lane.)

⑥ (35.5km/22.0mi)   After descending the long, steep hill and bearing R at the bottom (with Sooke Lake Road going to the L), you turn L onto West Shawnigan Lake Road. You'll now circumnavigate the lake in a clockwise direction.

⑦ (44.6km/27.7mi)   The road terminates at a stop sign, where you turn R onto Renfrew Road.

⑧ (49.4km/30.7mi)   Continue on through the centre of Shawnigan Lake village onto Shawnigan Lake Road.

⑨ (57.0km/35.4mi)   Leaving the lake you now retrace your route, bearing L up the 6km/3.7mi hill of Shawnigan Lake Road to the Trans-Canada Highway (aka Malahat Drive).

⑩ (63.0km/39.1mi)   Turn R onto the highway.

⑪ (81.9mk/50.9mi)   Turn R onto the well-signed Exit 11 View Royal/Colwood off-ramp. At the bottom of the ramp turn R onto Six Mile Road, and after 200m/yd turn L onto Atkins Road (signed for

the Galloping Goose Regional Trail).
As Atkins ends continue onto the
Galloping Goose Trail and ride its
10km/6.2mi length back to Victoria to
finish at the Johnson Street Bridge.

Along The Malahat.

PART TWO: DUNCAN AND COWICHAN VALLEY

The "City of Totems" is how Duncan proclaims itself to the world. Which is appropriate, as the city is dotted with large, skillfully carved and painted totem poles crafted by the Cowichan First Nation's gifted artisans. There are 38 poles in all and each one tells a story of the carver's tribal family.

The Cowichan Tribes have the largest First Nation population in BC and their presence in the valley goes back to time immemorial. Quw'ulsun' is the First Nation's name in their own language, which means, appropriately, "sun warming the back" or simply "the warm land." The Quw'ulsun' are a dynamic and industrious people who, among many other enterprises, once owned the Cherry Point Vineyards.

Duncan is the commercial centre of the Cowichan Valley, and its century-old town hall presides over a bustling downtown core of stores and small businesses. The rides that are described here start from the local museum. Not far from the town hall, the museum is housed in an even older building: the town's 1912 train station. Its exhibits tell the history of the valley's Indigenous people and its early white settlers.

The place was originally named Alderlea. That was the name of William Chalmers Duncan's farm, which the Esquimalt & Nanaimo Railway cut across when it was built in 1886. The land was referred to as Duncan's Crossing. A year later, when a train station was built, it was called Duncan's Station. It took until 1926 before the post office dropped the "station" part of the name and it became simply Duncan.

(Actually, the city of Duncan is the smallest, by area, in Canada.)

Because of its "warm land" climate, the surrounding countryside is a winsome concoction of farmland, vineyards, picturesque homes and gardens, lakes, cozy bays, small villages (and seductive cafés) and a very compact and friendly town that provides us cyclists with the almost unassailable reason for a pedalling visit.

And that's why there are three routes to choose from. The north and south loops are two separate rides. The third route is a combination of the two. In a sense, it completes the circle – the Tour of Duncan.

tourismcowichan.com

duncan.ca

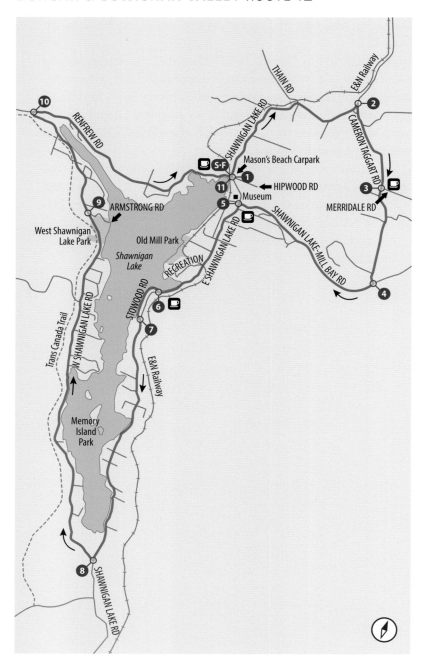

Mason's Beach Carpark

HIPWOOD RD

Museum

ARMSTRONG RD

West Shawnigan
Lake Park

Old Mill Park

Shawnigan
Lake

RECREATION

Trans Canada Trail

W SHAWNIGAN LAKE RD

STOWOOD RD

E&N Railway

Memory
Island
Park

RENFREW RD

THAIN RD

E&N Railway

CAMERON TAGGART RD

SHAWNIGAN LAKE RD

MERRIDALE RD

SHAWNIGAN LAKE-MILL BAY RD

E SHAWNIGAN LAKE RD

SHAWNIGAN LAKE RD

S·F

Shawnigan Lake /
Cameron Taggart Loop

Shawnigan Lake has always been a favourite spot for Islanders to visit. The private Shawnigan Lake School has occupied its ivy-covered main buildings set amongst formal gardens since 1916. You'll get a glimpse of the school about a kilometre/0.6 mile from the end of the ride.

At the Lake's village you'll find a museum dedicated to the pioneering spirit of the area, and a small array of stores and cafés. Cameron Taggart Road, besides being a lovely bucolic backroad, is the only way to the province's first estate cidery. The Merridale Cidery and Distillery, at the end of Merridale Road, is reputed to produce "the best English-style cider in Canada." Like their cousins the local vineyards, Merridale offers cider and spirit tastings in a rustic farmhouse and gives tours of the orchard, apple mills, presses and fermentation casks. It also has an "eatery."

West of the lake is an abandoned CN railway line (now part of the Cowichan Valley Trail, aka the Trans Canada Trail. For the railway to span the Koksilah River, a huge trestle was constructed in 1920 which still has the reputation as being one of the world's highest and longest. Known as the Kinsol Trestle, it's now a popular tourist attraction and is the start of ride 15 that takes you to Lake Cowichan.

DISTANCE	32km/20mi or 22km/13.5mi.
LEVEL	Moderate.
HIGHLIGHTS	Beautiful lake; rural road with light traffic; West Shawnigan Lake Provincial Park with beach and picnic area; possible visit to a cidery, distillery and vineyard; possible side trip to the Kinsol Trestle.
START	Mason's Beach parking area 0.5km/550yd north of Shawnigan Lake Village.

From Victoria (Shawnigan Lake is 45km/28mi northwest of Victoria): Take Douglas Street/Trans-Canada Highway out of town. Continue on the highway up and over the Malahat to Mill Bay. At the second set of traffic lights turn L onto Shawnigan Lake–Mill Bay Road. After 9km/5.5mi and at the junction with Shawnigan Lake Road in Shawnigan Lake Village turn R onto Shawnigan Lake Road. After 0.5km/550yd, turn R into the gravel parking area to Mason's Beach just before the intersection of Shawnigan Lake Road and Renfrew Road.

From Duncan (Shawnigan Lake is 19km/12mi southwest of Duncan): Take the Trans-Canada Highway out of town going south. After 12km/7.5mi turn R onto Cobble Hill Road at the traffic lights at the Cowichan Bay Road/Cobble Hill Road intersection. Continue straight at the village of Cobble Hill as the road becomes Shawnigan Lake Road. After 7km/4.3mi turn L at a major junction onto a continuation of Shawnigan Lake Road and then immediately L into a gravel parking area (also the entrance to Hipwood Road).

The route

①		From the parking area turn R onto Shawnigan Lake Road, then R again onto a continuation of Shawnigan Lake Road. (For a shorter ride – by 10km/6mi and avoiding the Cameron Taggart loop – turn L out of the start's parking area to ride the 0.5km/550yd to the village and circumnavigate the lake clockwise (see segment 5 below).
②	(3.2 km/2.0mi)	Turn R onto Cameron Taggart Road. After 50m/yd continue R on the same road.

③ (5.0 km/3.1mi)   To the L is Merridale Road, the location of the Merridale Estate Cider and Distillery. A short distance farther is the Unsworth Vineyards. Both serve food and are worth a visit.

④ (6.9 km/4.3mi)   Turn R onto Shawnigan Lake–Mill Bay Road.

⑤ (10.0 km/6.2mi)   At Shawnigan Lake Village turn L at the stop sign onto Shawnigan Lake Road.

⑥ (12.4 km/7.5mi)   Less than a kilometre/0.6 mile after passing under a railway bridge, turn R onto a lakeside road. You'll avoid a nasty hill this way. Also, you'll pass a restaurant and marina – if you're interested in a bite to eat – and lakeside cottages.

⑦ (13.3 km/8.3mi)   Turn R to rejoin the main road.

⑧ (18.1 km/11.2mi)   At the end of the lake turn R onto West Shawnigan Lake Road.

⑨ (24.9 km/15.5mi)   On the R is the entrance to West Shawnigan Lake Provincial Park.

⑩ (27.5 km/17.1mi)   Turn R onto Renfrew Road. (To view the Kinsol Trestle, billed as one of the world's longest and highest trestles, turn L here and ride the 1.9km/1.2mi to Glen Eagles Road and turn R. Then follow the signs for the trestle, a further 2km/1.2mi, mostly on good gravel.)

⑪ (31.9 km/19.8mi)   Ride past Mason's Beach on your R and the grocery store and junction with Shawnigan Lake Road on the L, and turn L into the Mason's Beach parking area.

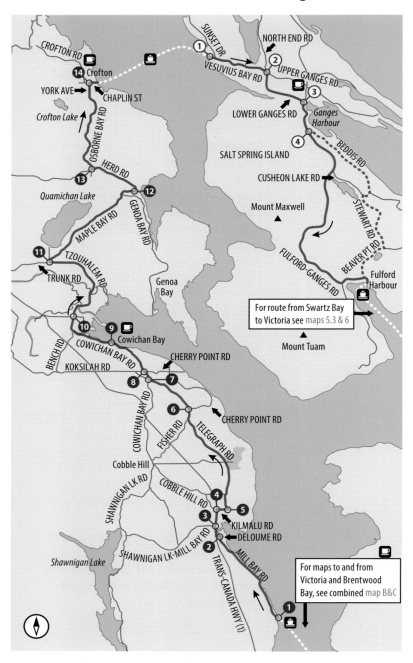

For route from Swartz Bay to Victoria see maps 5.3 & 6

For maps to and from Victoria and Brentwood Bay, see combined map B&C

Three Ferries Loop (Victoria / Crofton / Salt Spring Island / Victoria)

At the end of the Saanich Peninsula, Salt Spring Island rises from the surrounding waters like a rocky promontory that seems too irresistible not to explore. The quickest and easiest way to do that, if you live in or are visiting Victoria is to ride or drive out to the Swartz Bay ferry terminal and jump on the ferry to Fulford Harbour at the Island's south end. But, over many years, local cyclists have adopted a more contrary route to visiting the Island. Salt Spring has three ferry terminals: Vesuvius on its northwest coast, Long Harbour on its east coast and Fulford Harbour in the south. For contrary cyclists the Vesuvius ferry trip has more appeal. The journey to Crofton, where the ferry to Vesuvius departs, offers a more satisfying and varied, albeit longer, ride and is, in a literal sense, part of a good day's outing.

The three ferries included in this route are Brentwood Bay–Mill Bay; Crofton–Vesuvius and Fulford Harbour–Swartz Bay, and each plies a disparate part of the inner waters of the Salish Sea, i.e., Saanich Inlet, Stuart Channel and Satellite Channel respectively.

The beauty of this circuitous route is the opportunity to stop and explore some of the area's smaller but interesting communities. Cowichan Bay is a good example. Its collection of waterfront homes, stores, cafes and restaurants plus its marinas make it a worthwhile stop for coffee and snacks and for some nosing about. Crofton, while not as alluring as Cowichan Bay, does have a small museum, a pub/cafe and a pleasant waterfront trail that is easily accessed. Ganges, on Salt Spring Island, has much to reward your curiosity. It has a good selection of cafes and restaurants. It also has an eclectic bookstore, a couple of art galleries, two grocery stores, a pub, an intriguing hardware store and a waterfront park that, on summer Saturdays, has an outdoor market not to be missed if you can help it.

On this route, make sure to allow enough time so you won't miss your planned ferry departure.

bcferries.com

DISTANCE	113km/70mi.
LEVEL	Moderate to strenuous.
HIGHLIGHTS	Ferry rides and views of Saanich Inlet, Stuart Channel and Satellite Channel; Cowichan Bay village; Cowichan Valley's pastoral landscapes; Salt Spring Island sights; Ganges restaurants, pub, stores and park; Saanich Peninsula farmlands.
START	Johnson Street Bridge, downtown Victoria.

The route

To ferry 1: Victoria to Brentwood Bay

①		Cross the bridge on the signed Galloping Goose Regional Trail and bear R onto Harbour Road for 400 or so metres/yards. Then turn R to continue on the "Goose" to its junction with the Lochside Trail at the Switch Bridge.
②	(4.0km/2.5mi)	At the Switch Bridge turn L onto the continuation of the "Goose."
③	(4.8km/3.mi)	Cross traffic-lighted Tillicum Road, keeping to the paved trail. After about 100m/yd and just before a trestle bridge, turn R down a marked short but steep trail and turn R again

onto the bike lane of Interurban Road.

④ (10.5km/6.5mi) After passing through two sets of traffic lights, and at the end of Interurban, turn L at the light onto West Saanich Road.

⑤ (14.0km/8.7mi) Just past a market garden store on your L, turn L onto Wallace Drive. Be cautious here as you cross oncoming traffic on West Saanich Road.

⑥ (18.5km/11.5mi) About 600m/yd after having crossed Benvenuto Avenue (which is the access road to Butchart Gardens), turn L onto Hagen Road.

⑦ (19.0km/11.8mi) Turn L onto Marchant Road. Follow Marchant as it swings R to become Brentwood Drive.

⑧ (20.0km/12.4mi) At the end of Brentwood Drive turn L onto Verdier Avenue to ride the short distance down to the ferry terminal.

The ferry to Mill Bay takes about 25 minutes, running every hour or so from 7:30 a.m. to 5:55 p.m. daily. Check the schedule at bcferries.com.

To ferry 2: Mill Bay to Crofton

① Once you've disembarked from the ferry, ride the 200 m/yd up to Mill Bay Road and turn R.

② (5.2km/3.2mi) Ride past the Mill Bay shopping centre (L) and at the stop sign turn L onto Deloume Road.

③ (5.4km3.3mi) As Deloume intersects the Trans-Canada Highway bear R onto the northbound highway's shoulder.

④	(6.4km/4mi)	At the second set of traffic lights turn R onto Kilmalu Road.
⑤	(7.2km/4.5mi)	At the top of the first rise turn L onto Telegraph Road.
⑥	(13.4km/8.3mi)	Pass Cherry Point Road. Its eponymous winery is a kilometre on the L.
⑦	(16.1km/10mi)	At the first junction turn R onto Cowichan Bay Road.
⑧	(17.0km/10.5mi)	Pass the intersection of Koksilah and Cherry Point roads. You soon start your descent of a 15 per cent and then 12 per cent hill into Cowichan Bay.
⑨	(18.3km/11.4mi)	Begin your ride through the seaside village of Cowichan Bay.
⑩	(22.1km/13.7mi)	Continue straight on Tzouhalem

Cowichan Bay.

Road as Cowichan Bay Road turns abruptly L.

⑪ (27.3km/17mi)   Turn R at a large roundabout onto Maple Bay Road.

⑫ (33.4km/20.7mi)   Almost at the bottom of a steep hill (and just before Maple Bay itself) turn L onto Herd Road. This is signed for Crofton and the Salt Spring Island ferry.

⑬ (35.1km/21.8mi)   The next major thoroughfare, on your R, is Osborne Bay Road (also signed for Crofton and Salt Spring Island). Turn R here.

⑭ (40.3km/25.0mi)   As Osborne Bay Road intersects Chaplin Street in Crofton, turn R onto Chaplin to ride the 400m/yd down to the ferry terminal.

The ferry from Crofton to Vesuvius on Salt Spring Island runs frequently and takes about 25 minutes. Check bcferries.com for schedules.

To ferry 3: Crofton to Salt Spring Island

①   Disembark from the ferry and turn R onto Vesuvius Bay Road. After 500m/yd pass Sunset Drive on your L. (Sunset Drive is the long way to Ganges, Salt Spring's main centre.)

② (3.5km/2.2mi)   At a four-way stop sign turn R onto Lower Ganges Road. North End Road goes L and Upper Ganges Road is straight ahead.

③ (7.2km/4.5mi)   After descending the steep and curving Lower Ganges Road into Ganges (a great place to stop and eat or at least poke-about) you turn R onto Fulford–Ganges Road. Centennial Park is straight ahead.

④ (21.2km/13.2mi) Fulford–Ganges Road is rather like a humpback whale: it rises for half its length and descends for the other half. The road ends at the Fulford Harbour ferry terminal, for your next ferry ride.

For an alternative route to Fulford Harbour, take Beddis Road, on your L at 1.3km/0.8mi from Centennial Park on Fulford–Ganges Road, and after 5km/3mi turn R onto Cusheon Lake Road. Then take the first L onto Stewart Road (an up-and-over road) for about 4km/2.5mi. As Stewart meets Beaver Point Road at a stop sign, turn R onto Beaver Point Road and ride down to its junction with Fulford–Ganges Road. Turn L here and descend the 300m/yd to the ferry terminal. Although a slightly harder route, it's also a fraction shorter than the main route.

The ferry from Fulford Harbour to Swartz Bay runs fairly frequently and takes approximately 40 minutes. Check bcferries.com for times.

Swartz Bay Ferry Terminal to Victoria

Leaving the ferry, follow the terminal roadway exit signs (bike decals on the pavement also indicate the way). After about 400m/yd and an overpass you can either:

A: Continue as the road becomes the Pat Bay Highway (17) riding the 30-odd kilometres/18-plus miles on the highway's wide shoulder to Victoria. The highway becomes Blanshard Street on the outskirts of town. In town, turn R onto Pandora Avenue and return to the ride's start at the bridge.

or

B: Take the Lochside Trail to Victoria. After disembarking

from the ferry, stay on the exit road, and after passing under an overpass, look for and take a cycle path rising sharply to your R. Follow this path as it turns R and then R again, going over the overpass and onto Lands End Road. At the traffic lights, cross over onto Kittiwake Place. After 50m/yd turn R onto Curteis Road and follow the Lochside Trail signs for 32km/20mi to Victoria. (There are some sections of good gravel on this trail.)

(For more detail, see map of ferry exit route on p312)

NOTE: The Lochside Trail joins the Galloping Goose Trail at the Switch Bridge (which crosses the Trans-Canada Highway) with 4km/2.5mi remaining of the route. The Johnson Street Bridge marks the end of the trail.

Arriving at Mill Bay.

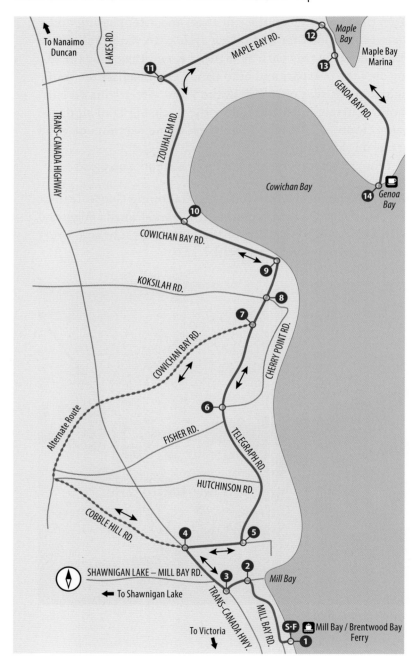

Mill Bay Ferry Terminal to Genoa Bay

This out-and-back ride from the Mill Bay ferry terminal takes you to Genoa Bay, a small inlet off Cowichan Bay at the south end of Sansum Narrows. Genoa Bay is a tiny, end-of-the-road settlement with a cozy marina. It was named by a homesick Italian pioneer of the area because, he said, it reminded him of his home in Italy. That was in 1858. Anyone who's been to the Italian Genoa might find the resemblance a considerable stretch. But, to a romantically inclined Italian thousands of kilometres from home, the bay might have provoked some nostalgic longing for the historic port city. (Incidentally, just in case you didn't know – and I'm sure you do – Genoa was the birthplace of Christopher Columbus. He set sail from southern Spain to establish a new route to the East Indies but wound up "discovering" the "new world" instead.)

Although the route is a trifle lumpy, the ride is a gem. The ups and downs are compensated by the ride through Cowichan Bay and the views over coastal waters, protected coves, pastoral land and the wooded slopes of local hills and Mt. Tzouhalem.

DISTANCE	82km/51mi out and back.
LEVEL	Moderate to strenuous.
HIGHLIGHTS	Ferry ride; possible winery visits; coffee and munchies in Cowichan Bay village; bucolic road to Genoa Bay; lunch at Maple Bay Marina or Genoa Bay Café; possible visit to Maple Bay village.
START	Mill Bay ferry terminal (ride or take your car to the ferry terminal at Brentwood Bay. The directions from Victoria to the Brentwood Bay ferry are on p315. For the return to Victoria, the Mill Bay–Brentwood Bay Ferry, p318, runs fairly frequently. See fares and schedules at bcferries.com.

The route

①   From the ferry terminal's entrance turn R onto Mill Bay Road.

② (5.2km/3.2mi)   Ride past the shopping centre (L) and at the stop sign turn L onto Deloume Road.

③ (5.4km3.3mi)   As Deloume intersects the Trans-Canada Highway bear R onto the northbound highway's shoulder and onto the highway.

④ (6.4km/4mi)   At the second set of traffic lights turn R onto Kilmalu Road.

⑤ (7.2km/4.5mi)   At the top of the first rise turn L onto Telegraph Road.

⑥ (13.4km/8.3mi)   Pass Cherry Point Road. Its eponymous winery is a kilometre on the L.

⑦ (16.1km/10mi)   At the first junction turn R onto Cowichan Bay Road.

⑧ (17.0km/10.5mi)   Pass the intersection of Koksilah and Cherry Point roads. You soon start your descent of a 15 per cent and then 12 per cent hill into Cowichan Bay. (You'll remember this grade on your way back!)

⑨ (18.3km/11.4mi)   Begin your ride through the seaside village of Cowichan Bay.

⑩ (22.1km/13.7mi)   Continue straight on Tzouhalem Road as Cowichan Bay Road turns abruptly L.

⑪ (27.3km/17mi)   Turn R at a large roundabout onto Maple Bay Road.

⑫ (32.8km/20.4mi)   After a hilly 5.3km/3.3mi ride, turn R onto Genoa Bay Road. (Genoa Bay is now only 8km/5mi away.)

⑬ (35.8km/22.2mi) Pass Maple Bay Marina on your L.

⑭ (41.2km/25.6mi) Follow the road as it bears L into Genoa Bay with its marina, store, café/restaurant and salubrious restrooms.

Return to the Mill Bay ferry

On your way back you could drop down into Maple Bay itself. If you do, look for and take Chisholm Trail on your R just before the final hill going up to Maple Bay Road and about 1km/0.6mi before the junction with Maple Bay Road. At the stop sign, turn R onto Redcap Street and ride down to turn L onto Beaumont Avenue. This is downtown Maple Bay. To return to Maple Bay Road, retrace to just before Chisholm Trail and turn sharp R onto Drummond Drive opposite a kayaking outfit. After 50m/yd bear L onto Maple Bay Road. All the above is steep terrain but is encompassed within just a couple of kilometres/one mile.

Genoa Bay.

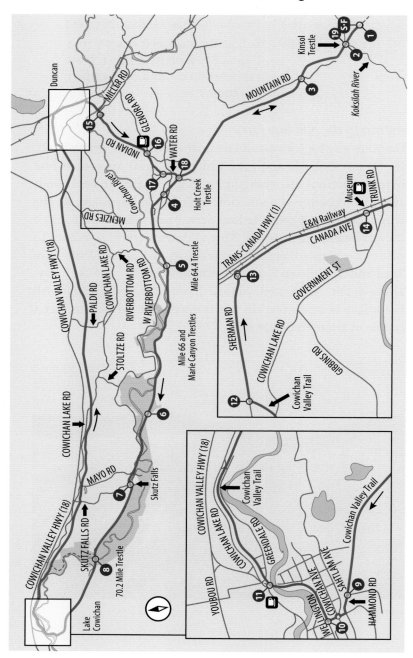

Kinsol Trestle / Lake Cowichan / Duncan / Glenora Loop

When I first saw the Kinsol Trestle it was in a sorry state. The year was 1999. I had ridden my old mountain bike as far as I could on the little used, little known Cowichan Valley Trail from south Shawnigan. The trestle looked old. Moss covered many of its timbers. Decay was ravaging many more. Its graceful arc was marred by a blackened hole where vandals had torched the rail bed years before. A huge sign warned me to "KEEP OUT" and that the structure was "UNSTABLE." In the intervening years, due to the persistence, diligence and mindfulness of the people of the valley, the almost century-old trestle has risen, phoenix-like, to be the structure we see and use today. Its aesthetic form and complexity of construction have delighted and awed countless visitors since its reopening in the summer of 2011. And you'll be one of them.

The Cowichan Valley Trail itself is as flat as a pancake and the surface is mostly of reasonable quality gravel. There is a mixture of wide and single track and there's one short section from the Kinsol Trestle, about a quarter of the way out to Lake Cowichan, that's always wet and muddy. Roughly 10km/6mi from the lake is the access to Skutz Falls, a nice, short detour from the linear, park-like trail. And there are enough crossings of the Cowichan River to remind you of its proximity.

Although I've created a large loop route, you can stop and return at any point on the trail out to Lake Cowichan. The loop described here incorporates both the south and north portions of the Cowichan Valley Trail (now also known as a segment of the Trans Canada Trail) that travels on both sides of the Cowichan River. It takes you very close to Duncan's town centre and out to the pastoral lands around the hamlet of Glenora southwest of town. The route takes you into the heart of the Cowichan Valley's western aspect and gives a good sense of the variety of its character.

DISTANCE	84km/52mi.
LEVEL	Easy to moderate.
HIGHLIGHTS	Kinsol Trestle; trestles crossing the Cowichan River; semi-isolated, park-like trail that's never far from the Cowichan River; Skutz Falls and Cowichan River Provincial Park; possible visit to Lake Cowichan; downtown Duncan; the hamlet of Glenora and its neighbouring vineyards.
HOW TO GET THERe	From Shawnigan Lake village head north and then west on Renfrew Road for 7km/4.3mi and turn R onto Glen Eagles Road. After 400m/yd turn R into the parking area for the Kinsol Trestle trailhead. (These directions assume you've already driven up and over the Malahat on Highway 1 and arrived at the village via Shawnigan Lake Road (South) or on the Shawnigan Lake–Mill Bay Road.)
START	The Kinsol Trestle at its trailhead at the Glen Eagles Road parking area.

The route

① Leave the parking area on the wide and well-groomed gravel Cowichan Valley Trail going north.

② (1.3km/800yds) Ride over the impressive, 187-metre/204-yard-long Kinsol Trestle.

③ (4.2km/2.6mi) Cross the gravel Mountain Road.

④ (15.4km/9.6mi) Cross the Holt Creek Trestle.

⑤ (23.2km/14.4mi) Cross the 64.4 Mile Trestle. (This is the first of the trestles spanning the Cowichan River on the way to Lake Cowichan.)

⑥ (26.0km/16mi)   Cross the Mile 66 Trestle, aka Marie Canyon Trestle. (The "mile" designations are a relic from when the trail was a rail line and part of the Canadian North Pacific Railway. The figure denotes the distance from the line's start in Victoria.)

⑦ (29.0km/10mi)   Pass the entrance to Skutz Falls in Cowichan River Provincial Park.

⑧ (32.5km/20.2mi)   Cross the Mile 70.2 Trestle.

⑨ (36.5km/22.7mi)   The trail becomes Hammond Road here and you're on the outskirts of Lake Cowichan. After a very short distance turn R onto King George Street to ride to and cross a roundabout, keeping to King George Street.

⑩ (36.7km/22.9mi)   Less than 50m/yd after the roundabout, turn R onto a continuation of the Cowichan Valley Trail that runs between Nelson Road and Wellington Road.

⑪ (37.7km/23.4mi)   After crossing an old truss bridge over the Cowichan River, take the L fork in the trail to then cross Greendale Road onto the trail again. (You can detour here to explore the small town of Lake Cowichan, which is to your L a few hundred metres/ yards back on Cowichan Lake Road.) You now keep on this flat, well-maintained trail until the outskirts of Duncan, 25.3km/15.7mi away. (There is one steep gully to cross (Holmes Creek Trestle) about 1 km/0.5mi from the trail's end.)

⑫ (63.0km/39.1mi)   Turn R onto Sherman Road. This a
                       mostly downhill road taking you
                       toward downtown Duncan.

⑬ (64.0km/39.8mi)   Sherman ends at a roundabout. You
                       turn R onto Canada Avenue. This
                       takes you to the edge of downtown
                       Duncan.

⑭ (65.7km/40.8mi)   Just past the town's old railway
                       station (now a museum), turn R at a
                       traffic light onto Government Street
                       and immediately move to the left-
                       hand side of the road. After 20m/
                       yd turn L at a stop sign onto the
                       unmarked Underwood Street. After
                       another 20m/yd turn L at a stop sign,
                       onto Allenby Road.

⑮ (66.4km/41.2mi)   After crossing the Cowichan River
                       truss bridge, continue straight at the
                       four-way stop onto Indian Road. This
                       road starts with a steep, 15 per cent
                       ramp, then is more gently hilly until
                       the next checkpoint.

⑯ (69.9km/43.4mi)   At a four-way stop sign turn R onto
                       Glenora Road. This junction is the
                       hamlet of Glenora. It has a store and
                       café on the R before the turn. (Close
                       by are the plantings and winery of
                       Zanatta Vineyards.)

⑰ (71.2km/44.2mi)   After passing Elliot, Vaux and Rowe
                       roads, all on your R, bear L onto
                       Water Road, which crosses from the
                       R.

⑱ (71.7km/44.5mi)   A short distance along Water Road,
                       on your L, look for and take a gravel
                       trail going to your L. (A yellow metal
                       gate bars motor access.) You are now

back on the Cowichan Valley Trail and retracing your ride back to the Kinsol Trestle.

⑲ (82.7km/51.4km)   Cross the trestle and ride back to the route's start at the Glen Eagles Road parking area.

Top: *The Kinsol Trestle.*
Bottom: *Late autumn along the trail.*

Tour of Duncan – Combined Loop

DISTANCE	58km/36mi
LEVEL	Moderate

This route description differs from the book's usual format in that it's a combination of two routes – the south and north loops. My suggested direction for the whole Tour of Duncan is clockwise, starting with the south loop. At checkpoint 13 turn R onto Maple Bay Road and follow the north loop's checkpoints starting at 4. Of course, the accumulated distances between checkpoints will be different but you can make adjustments as you ride the northern loop.

START	Use the descriptions and maps for route 17 Tour of Duncan (South Loop) and route 18 Tour of Duncan (North Loop)

Bottom: *A glimpse of Somenos Lake.*
Opposite: *A couple of downtown Duncan's famous totem poles.*

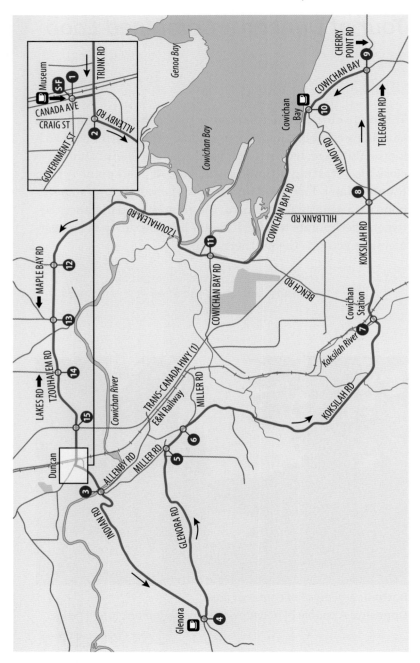

Tour of Duncan – South Loop

The village of Cowichan Bay is, without contest, the centre-piece of this meandering loop. Looking out over the waters of its bay and the larger Satellite Channel beyond, it's obvious that this village is a centre of marine activities. You can kayak from here. Go fishing, from wharf or skiff. Mosey around the Maritime Centre with its collection of antique boats. Picnic in bayside Hecate Park just up the road from the village. Perhaps best of all, you can sit and relax in one of the village's cafes or restaurants (the bakery is a favourite of mine) and then stroll along the wharfs, taking in the sights.

The other "Cowichan" on this ride is Cowichan Station. As the name implies, it was a stop on the E&N railway's journey from Victoria to Courtenay and back. The line was decommissioned in 2011 but the tiny station building is still intact and well looked after. The hamlet itself is rather quaint, and the narrow bridge over which the railway ran and the road goes under is a pleasant reminder of days gone by.

Providence Farm on Tzouhalem Road is another reminder of the past. Started as a farm and then purchased in 1864 by a Roman Catholic order of nuns, the Sisters of St. Ann, as a boarding school for First Nation girls, it is now a therapeutic community centre offering programs based on horticultural and vocational training principles. It's open to the public and has a store selling organic veggies and snacks.

DISTANCE	32km/20mi.
LEVEL	Moderate.
HIGHLIGHTS	Glenora, Cowichan Station and Cowichan Bay villages; Tzouhalem's St Anne's church and graveyard; Providence Farm; rural countryside; vineyards; bayside road.
START	Cowichan Valley Museum on Canada Avenue, downtown Duncan.

The route

①   From the museum ride south to Government Street and turn R. Ride to the L of Government for 25m/yd to a stop sign. Cross over onto Underwood Street.

② (200m/yd)   Turn L onto Allenby Road.

③ (1.0km/0.6mi)   Cross the bridge over the Cowichan River to a stop sign. Continue straight onto Indian Road. (This is a grunt for the first 700m/yd, but then it flattens out.)

④ (4.5km/2.8mi)   Turn L onto Glenora Road at the Glenora Store and Café. (Marshall Road goes straight ahead. Zanatta Winery is 250m/yd on the L on Marshall. For an additional 3.5km/2.2mi loop you could continue on Marshall Road, turn R onto Cavin Road, then R again on Waters Road and R again onto Glenora Road back to the store and café.)

⑤ (7.9km/4.9mi)   Turn R onto Miller Road.

⑥ (8.4km/5.2mi)   Turn R onto Koksilah Road.

⑦ (13.9km/8.6mi)   After crossing a truss bridge over the Koksilah River you pass under a railway bridge and through the tiny community of Cowichan Station. (For railway enthusiasts, turn R after the bridge onto Cowichan Station Road. This takes you past the small station building (R) and then back onto Koksilah Road, a matter of 250m/yd.)

Crossing the Koksilah River.

⑧	(15.8km/9.8mi)	Cross the Trans-Canada Highway, keeping to Koksilah Road.
⑨	(18.3km/11.4mi)	At a four-way intersection turn L onto Cowichan Bay Road.
⑩	(20.0km/12.4mi)	After a longish downhill you pass through the waterfront village of Cowichan Bay with its interesting stores, cafés and marinas.
⑪	(23.5km/14.6mi)	As Cowichan Bay Road turns abruptly L you continue straight on what is now named Tzouhalem Road.
⑫	(27.1km/16.3mi)	Pass St. Ann's Church and Providence Farm on your R.
⑬	(28.6km/17.8mi)	Continue on Tzouhalem Road at the roundabout. Maple Bay Road goes to the R. (For those riding the complete Tour of Duncan, turn R here onto Maple Bay Road and follow the description for the northern section of the tour on p124, checkpoint 4)
⑭	(29.6km/18.4mi)	Pass the junction with Lakes Road (R). Tzouhalem now becomes Trunk Road. Keep to Trunk Road, following its bends into town.
⑮	(30.8km/19.1mi)	Cross the Trans-Canada Highway and ride the remaining 600m/yd back to Canada Avenue and the museum.

Top: *Mt. Tzouhalem.*
Bottom: *Downtown Duncan.*

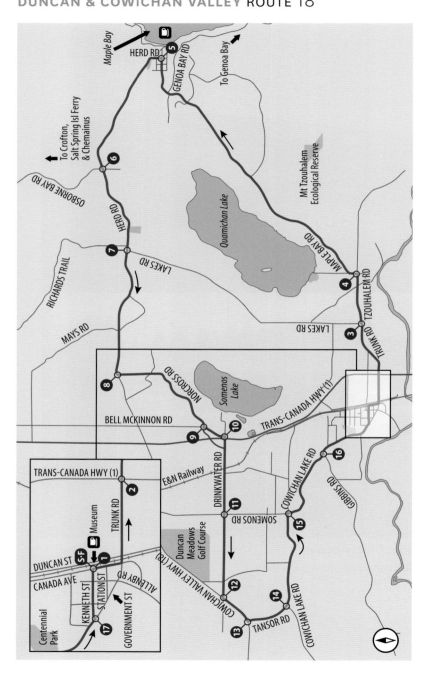

Tour of Duncan – North Loop

It's hard to pick one road that typifies this part of the Cowichan Valley. But if I had to, I'd go for Norcross Road. As described below, it runs 2.2km/1.3mi cross-country from Herd Road to Bill McKinnon Road, and while not flat it has no steep hills to speak of. What it does have, though, is a spectrum of rural scenes that will captivate even the most hardened of urban riders. There are views of surrounding high ground: Mt. Prevost to the west and Mt. Maple and Mt. Tzouhalem to the east. There are even views of Somenos Lake if you know where to look. The road is lined with a fusion of sloping vineyards, open pastures and parades of both deciduous and coniferous trees. Its collection of hobby farms, country homes large and small and a vineyard are a sign that a few discerning folks have given preference, over the years, to wanting to settle in such bucolic surroundings.

DISTANCE	29km/18mi.
LEVEL	Moderate.
HIGHLIGHTS	Rural roads; lakes and bays; farmland; vineyards; small farms; Cowichan Bay village's cafes, bakery and shops; downtown Duncan; possible side trip to Genoa Bay.
START	The Cowichan Valley Museum in the renovated Duncan railway station on Canada Avenue.

The route

①		From the museum, ride south to Government Street and turn L onto Trunk Road.
②	(650m/yd)	Continue on Trunk Road as it crosses the Trans-Canada Highway.
③	(2.2km/1.4mi)	Trunk Road becomes Tzouhalem

Road at its junction with Lakes Road (L). Continue straight.

④ (3.2km/2.0mi)   At a roundabout, turn L onto Maple Bay Road.

⑤ (9.3km/5.8mi)   After a long downhill and at a Crofton/Salt Spring Ferry sign (R), turn L onto Herd Road. Herd Road is slightly concealed, so be aware. (For an out-and-back ride to Genoa Bay, turn R 400m/yd before Herd Road onto the well-signed Genoa Bay Road. Add 16km/10mi to your ride. See route #14 Mill Bay Ferry to Genoa Bay).

⑥ (12.0km/7.5mi)   Pass Osborne Bay Road on your R. This road is signed for Crofton and the Salt Spring Island ferry.

⑦ (13.8km/8.6mi)   Pass Richards Trail on your R, then Lakes Road on your L. (This is a possible escape route back to Trunk Road and the ride's start.)

⑧ (16.4km/10.2mi)   Turn L onto Norcross Road on a short downhill. Norcross takes you through the quintessential North Cowichan Valley countryside: rural homes, small farms, open fields, vineyards (including Emandare Vineyards) and lake views.

⑨ (18.6km/11.5mi)   At a stop sign turn L onto Bill McKinnon Road.

⑩ (19.0km/11.8mi)   Bill McKinnon Road ends at the Trans-Canada Highway. (The BC Forest Discovery Centre is on the L at this intersection.) Cross the highway onto Drinkwater Road.

⑪ (20.5km/12.3mi)   At a second roundabout continue on Drinkwater.

⑫	(22.2km/13.8mi	Turn L at the next junction, onto Cowichan Valley Highway.
⑬	(22.9km/14.2mi)	As the highway bears R you turn L onto Tansor Road.
⑭	(23.8km/14.8mi)	After 900m/yd Tansor swings L to join and become Cowichan Lake Road.
⑮	(25.7km/16.0mi)	Turn R at the roundabout to continue on Cowichan Lake Road. (Somenos Road goes L and Sherman Road goes straight.)
⑯	(27.2km/16.9mi)	At yet another roundabout, continue straight as Cowichan Lake Road becomes Government Street.
⑰	(28.4km/17.6mi)	Soon after entering town, turn L onto either Kenneth or Station street and ride through the centre of downtown. Turn R as Kenneth (or Station) ends at Canada Avenue. The museum is a few metres/yards on the L.

A cycling vintner.

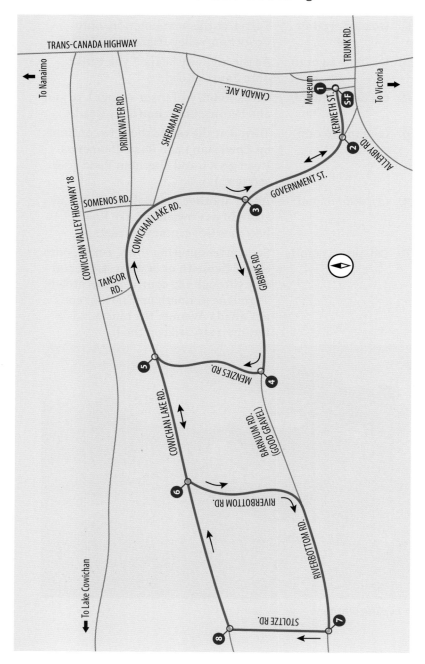

Tour of Duncan – *West Loop*

The defining feature of this ride, which is essentially the western tentacle of the much larger Cowichan Valley, is the Cowichan River, though it is mostly hidden from view. And it is this river that, over the past 10,000 years, has sculptured this broad valley and left it fertile and full of possibilities – for settlements, agriculture, vineyards and... recreational pursuits like cycling.

A good portion of the ride is on Riverbottom Road, a route that contorts itself as it follows the meandering Cowichan River and, as a consequence, is rather a lumpy one. Companions of the river are the linear Cowichan River Provincial Park, the 22km/15.5mi Cowichan River Footpath and the Cowichan Valley Trail, which is part of the Trans Canada Trail.

DISTANCE	34km/21mi.
LEVEL	Moderate.
HIGHLIGHTS	Short ride through Duncan's attractive downtown; winding country roads; vistas over nearby summits; possible visits to two riverside parks: Sandy Pool and Stoltz Pool.
START	Cowichan Valley Museum on Canada Avenue in downtown Duncan.

The route

① From the museum turn R onto Canada Avenue, then immediately L onto Kenneth Street. This is a prominent downtown thoroughfare where you'll pass city hall (R) and a surprisingly well-stocked bookstore (also on the R).

② (0.4km/0.2mi) As Kenneth Street meets Government Street turn R onto Government. Continue on Government as it climbs out of town.

③ (1.5km/0.9mi) At a roundabout take the second exit onto Gibbins Road. (Note the local hospital on your R, just in case!)

④ (6.4km/4.0mi) Gibbins bears L to become Barnjum Road (Menzies Road to the R). Keep on Barnjum to its junction with Riverbottom Road. Wake Lake Nature Reserve is on your R just before the corner.

⑤ (8.5km/5.3mi) Turn L onto Riverbottom Road. Riverbottom Road is a longish stretch of the route and, as the name suggests, you ride close to the Cowichan River. Though you rarely see the river from the road, there are two parks where you can see it close-up: Sandy Pool Regional Park at 14km/8.7mi and Stoltz Pool in Cowichan River Provincial Park at 19.4km/12mi. Both are a stone's throw from the route.

⑥ (18.3km/11.4mi) As Riverbottom Road bears slightly L and becomes gravel (there's also a large Cowichan River Provincial Park sign here), you turn R onto Stoltz Road.

⑦ (19.4km/12.0mi) At a stop sign turn R onto Cowichan Lake Road.

⑧ (31.7km/19.7mi) At a roundabout take the first R to continue on Cowichan Lake Road. At another roundabout keep straight (Gibbins goes R). The road soon becomes Government Street, a long downhill back into town. In town you then turn L onto Kenneth Street and finish at the museum.

Top: *A patriotic display.*
Bottom: *The Cowichan River.*

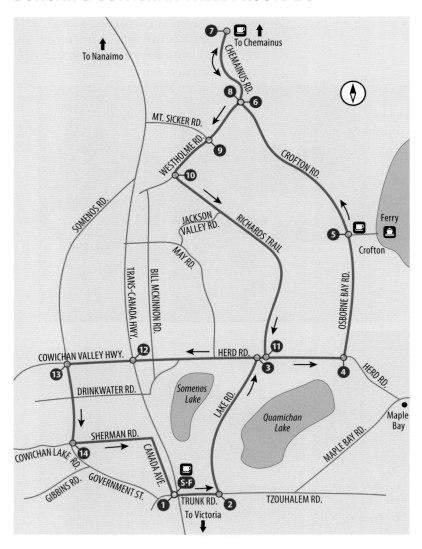

Duncan / Crofton / Chemainus Loop

Chemainus is one of those "pick yourself up, dust yourself off" kind of places that shouts to the world just how resilient the community is. With the downturn (some might say "demise") of the local lumber industry and the resulting economic effects in the early 1980s, the town decided to concentrate on tourism as a means of economic survival. Murals are now synonymous with Chemainus and they were its first major foray into the tourism industry. There are now over 40 murals scattered around the small town and, along with its successful live theatre, they attract thousands of visitors.

At almost 6km/3.7mi, Richards Trail is one of the longest roads on this ride. It's an old forestry access road to the nearby Mount Richards municipal forest and was named after an 1870s/80s councillor, Joseph Richards. Over the past many years, the trail has slowly been paved and the district settled by farmers and homesteaders. Today, with Mt. Richards towering on its eastern edge, it's a narrow, low traffic, gently twisting country road that's a treat to ride.

DISTANCE	50km/31mi.
LEVEL	Moderate.
HIGHLIGHTS	Chemainus and its murals; the village of Crofton; the bucolic Richards Trail; North Cowichan Valley farms and farmlands.
START	The Cowichan Valley Museum on Canada Avenue in downtown Duncan.

The route

①   From the museum go south along Canada Avenue to Government Street and turn L onto Trunk Road, riding toward the Trans-Canada Highway. Cross the highway, keeping to Trunk Road.

② (1.9km/1.1mi)   Turn L onto Lakes Road at the traffic lights.

③ (6.7km/4.2mi)   As Lakes Road ends turn R onto Herd Road.

④ (8.5km/5.3mi)   Turn L onto Osborne Bay Road, signed for Crofton and Salt Spring Ferry.

⑤ (13.7km/8.5mi)   After descending a long hill, ride through Crofton village to the road's junction with Chaplin Street and turn L. Ride 200m/yd and bear R onto Crofton Road. (Crofton is the BC Ferries terminal to Vesuvius on Salt Spring Island. It has a store, two pubs and a café.)

⑥ (17.5km/10.9mi)   As Crofton Road junctions Chemainus Road (aka Highway 1A) turn R to join Chemainus Road.

⑦ (23.0km/14.3mi)   Enter the town of Chemainus. Downtown is to your R. The ferry terminal for Thetis and Penelakut islands is at the end of Oak Street. Retrace your route back along Chemainus Road to checkpoint 6.

⑧ (28.5km/17.7mi)   Continue past Crofton Road on Chemainus Road.

⑨ (30.1km/18.7mi)   Bear L as Chemainus Road becomes the narrower Westholme Road. Mt. Sicker Road goes to the R, leading to the Trans-Canada Highway.

⑩ (32.6km/20.2mi)   Just before a long, curving R bend,

Top: *Feedstock for the Crofton pulp mill.*
Bottom: *Downtown Chemainus.*

Top: *Hockey night in Chemainus.*
Bottom: *Mt. Prevost overlooking Cowichan Valley farmland.*

look for and take Richards Trail. Don't worry, this road doesn't conform to the usual definition of a trail. It's a delightful, paved country road that meanders through long stretches of open farmland.

⑪ (38.5km/23.9mi)   At the stop sign turn R onto Herd Road. Continue on Herd to its junction with the Trans-Canada.

⑫ (42.6km/26.5mi)   Cross the highway onto the Cowichan Valley Highway (aka Highway 18).

⑬ (44.0km/27.3mi)   At a pedestrian crossing turn L onto Somenos Road.

⑭ (46.6km/29.0mi)   At a large roundabout turn L onto Sherman Road.

⑮ (48.4km/30.1mi)   Sherman ends at another roundabout. You turn R here onto Canada Avenue to ride the 1.6km/1.0mi back to the ride's start at the museum.

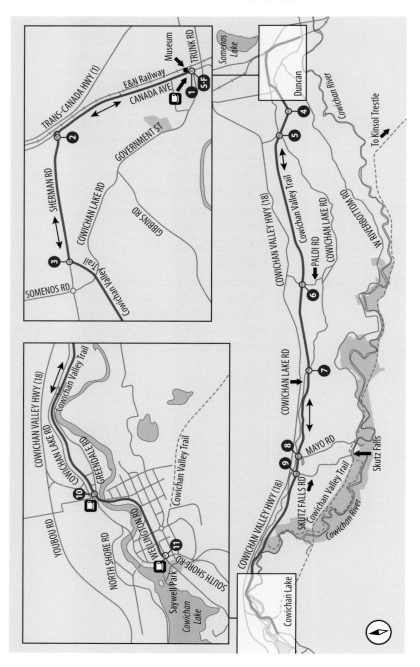

Cowichan Valley Trail (Duncan to Lake Cowichan out and back)

21

If you're looking for the easiest way to ride from Duncan to Lake Cowichan there's no doubting that the Cowichan Valley Trail is the way to go. Not only is it flat (railway grades typically are no more than 2 per cent at their steepest) and with a well-groomed gravel surface, it's a pleasure to ride. Once you leave Duncan's suburban streets and hit this converted railbed, you ride through long avenues of trees, traverse open fields and meadows, and most of the time you're enveloped in the quietude of the countryside.

This route is part of the grand national project called the Trans Canada Trail, which, when complete, will span 24,000 kilometres/15,000 miles from coast to coast. This 30km/19mi section can be described as a microcosm of that immense, multi-use cross-country corridor.

DISTANCE	60 km/37mi (out and back).
LEVEL	Easy.
HIGHLIGHTS	Linear trail that traverses farmland and meadows and travels through long avenues of trees; picnic on the shore of Cowichan Lake; pub refreshments at the lake, too.
START	The Cowichan Valley Museum on Canada Avenue in downtown Duncan. (Was once the town's E&N railway station.)

The route

①   From the museum ride north on Canada Avenue.

② (1.5km/1.0mi)   Turn L at the roundabout to take the unsigned Sherman Road.

137

③ (2.6km/1.6mi)   After a stiff kilometre/0.6-mile climb, turn L at a pedestrian crossing onto the beginning of the Cowichan Valley Trail.

④ (2.8km/1.7mi)   You descend steeply to cross the Holmes Creek Trestle. Despite what I said about the trail being flat, believe me, this is the only grunt work you'll have to do.

⑤ (3.0km/1.8mi)   Shortly after the creek, you cross Cowichan Lake Road.

⑥ (10.2km/8.3mi) Cross Paldi Road.

⑦ (12.5km/7.8mi) Cross Cowichan Lake Road a second time.

⑧ (21.1km/13.1mi) Cross Mayo Road.

⑨ (21.8km/13.5mi) Less than a kilometre/0.6 mile later, cross Skutz Falls Road. (Although this is a gravel road, if you turned L onto Skutz Falls Road, it would take you to Skutz Falls on the Cowichan River, 3km/1.8mi away.)

⑩ (28.9km/18mi)   The trail crosses Greendale Road on the outskirts of Lake Cowichan and bears L for 50m/yd before traversing a short trestle spanning the Cowichan River. The trail now threads its way through the side streets of the town for a short distance.

⑪ (30.1km/18.7mi) Trail's end. If you continue on Wellington Street for half a block you come to Saywell Park and the shores of Cowichan Lake. A short ride to your R is the town centre of Lake Cowichan.

Touring on the Cowichan Valley Trail.

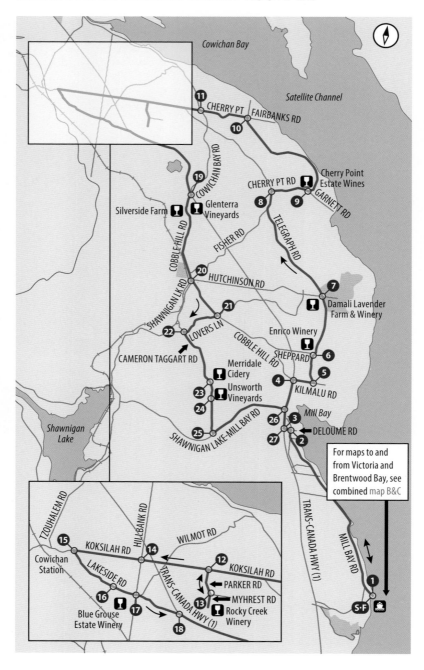

Cowichan Valley Winery Tour

Sunlight glinting on vine leaves. Row upon row of maturing, luscious grapes on vines rising like marshalled troops on the rolling hillside. The day's breeze tickling your arms and legs as you pedal along winding lanes. For all the world, you could be in Italy's Tuscan hills or France's Bordeaux region or even California's Napa Valley. But you're not. You're cycling through one of the continent's finest and fastest growing wine areas – the Cowichan Valley.

This tour will take you to seven of the region's vineyards, each with its own special attractions. Most will offer food as well as wine tastings. (You can also visit a cidery/distillery and a berry farm.)

The ride is about 40km/25mi long and can be accomplished nicely in a day (depending on your proclivity for wine tasting!). For those who want a more leisurely pace, there are a number of B&Bs en route.

The Cowichan Valley is also known for its large dairy farms and smaller hobby farms. Both make for beautiful scenery and give a sense you're in the heart of the country.

Wineries on this tour:
- Enrico Winery
- Damali Lavender Farm and Winery
- Cherry Point Estates Wines
- Rocky Creek Winery
- Blue Grouse Winery
- Glenterra Vineyards
- Unsworth Vineyards
- Silverside Farm and Merridale Cidery, while not wineries, are similar enterprises worth a visit.

DISTANCE   41km/25.5mi.

LEVEL	Easy to moderate.
HIGHLIGHTS	Vineyards; a cidery; what more do I need to say? Ha... for the most part there's light traffic; lots of rolling countryside and a couple of interesting small communities.
START	The Mill Bay ferry terminal. (This assumes you're riding from Victoria to Brentwood Bay and catching the ferry to Mill Bay. See Ferry and Airport Access Routes section C.

How to get there by car

From Duncan: At the intersection of Trunk Road and the Trans-Canada Highway turn onto the TCH and travel south for 19.0km/11.8mi to the Mill Bay Shopping Centre, just off the highway in Mill Bay. Park in the large parking lot. Begin the tour at checkpoint 2.

From Victoria: Leave town on the Trans-Canada Highway. After 42km/26mi turn R onto Deloume Road and R again into the Mill Bay Shopping Centre's large parking lot. Park here and begin the tour at checkpoint 2.

The route

①		From the Mill Bay ferry slip turn R onto Mill Bay Road.
②	(5.1km/3.2mi)	Just past the entrance to the Mill Bay Shopping Centre turn L onto Deloume Road.
③	(5.3km/3.3mi)	At the junction with the Trans-Canada Highway turn R keeping to the highway's wide shoulder.
④	(6.7km/4.2mi)	Turn R at the second traffic light onto Kilmalu Road.
⑤	(7.2km/4.5mi)	Turn L onto Telegraph Road.
⑥	(8.6km/5.3mi)	After almost 1.5km/1mi you reach the

first of the tour's wineries, Enrico, on your L.

(7) (9.7km/6.0mi) Another kilometre farther, also on L, is the Damali Lavender Farm and Winery. Its entrance is a short distance up Hutchinson Road.

(8) (13.3km/8.3mi) Turn R onto Cherry Point Road.

(9) (14.3km/8.9mi) A kilometre/0.6mi farther, on your L, is the Cherry Point Estate Wines.

(10) (17.8km/11.mi) Still on Cherry Point Road, turn sharp L. Although there are stop signs R and L and you have the right-of-way, be aware of traffic.

(11) (19.2km/11.9mi) At the stop sign, cross Cowichan Bay Road onto Koksilah Road.

(12) (20.9km/13.0mi) Turn L onto Parker Road. In summer months there's often a sandwich board at this corner, pointing to Rocky Creek Winery.

(13) (21.5km/13.4mi) Just after Parker morphs into Myhrest Road is the Rocky Creek Winery on your R. You now retrace the ride to the next checkpoint.

(14) (23.0km/14.3mi) Cross the Trans-Canada Highway to continue on Koksilah Road.

(15) (24.5km/15.2mi) At 100m/yd before the hamlet of Cowichan Station, turn L onto Lakeside Road. (There are no facilities in Cowichan Station, though some might find the well-preserved small station building interesting. Best seen from Cowichan Station Road, the first road on the R after the railway bridge.)

(16) (25.5km/15.8mi) The Blue Grouse Estate Winery is on

your R a short way along Lakeside Road. (Next to the winery is the Sunrise Waldorf School.)

⑰ (26.0km/16.1mi) Cross Hillbank Road at the four-way stop sign and then also cross Wilmot Road to continue on Lakeside. After a kilometre/0.6mi Lakeside bears R to run parallel to the Trans-Canada Highway.

⑱ (27.8km/17.3mi) At a stop sign turn L and then R to join the highway. Don't worry, you're only on this stretch of highway for a short while, and it has a wide shoulder with plenty of room for you.

⑲ (29.6km/18.4mi) Turn R at a major junction onto Cobble Hill Road. Half a kilometre/0.3mi along this road, on your L, are Glenterra Vineyards. A few hundred metres/yards farther, on the R, is Silverside Farm.

⑳ (32.2km/20.0mi) Having just passed the village of Cobble Hill, turn L onto a continuation of Cobble Hill Road.

㉑ (33.5km/20.8mi) Take the first turn on your R onto the quaintly named Lovers Lane. (No, it's not spelled with an apostrophe, although its abbreviation, Lvrs' Ln, is.)

㉒ (34.6km/21.5mi) At the end of Lovers Lane, turn L onto Cameron Taggart Road.

㉓ (35.8km/22.2mi) Turn L onto Merridale Road, at the end of which is the Merridale Cidery and Distillery a mere 400m/yd away.

㉔ (36.4km/22.6mi) Also on your L, a few hundred

One of Cowichan Valley's finest!

		metres/yards farther, is the entrance to Unsworth Vineyards.
㉕	(37.7km/23.4mi)	From the vineyards, continue on Cameron Taggart Road and turn L onto Shawnigan Lake–Mill Bay Road.
㉖	(40.0km/24.8mi)	Turn R onto the Trans-Canada Highway. The next turn is tricky as you need to turn L on Deloume Road back into Mill Bay. You either wait for a break in the traffic and ride to the L side of the highway and get into the L turning lane, or keep to the R and ride to the crosswalk at the traffic light and cross on Deloume to ride down to Mill Bay Road.
㉗	(40.8km/25.5mi)	Turn R onto Mill Bay Road to ride the 5km/3mi back to the Mill Bay ferry.

tourismcowichan.com
enricowinery.com
damali.ca
cherrypointestatewines.com
bluegrouse.ca
glenterravineyards.com
merridale.ca
unsworthvineyards.com

Top: *Fine dining, wine-tour style.*
Bottom: *Definitely wine country.*

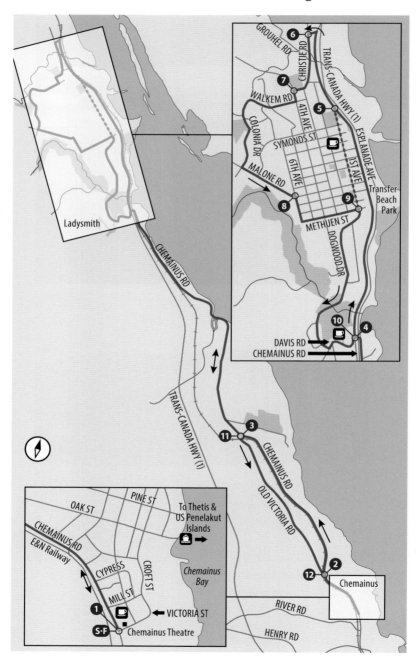

Chemainus to Ladysmith (out and back)

The Stz'uminus First Nation, who've inhabited this northern part of the Cowichan Valley for centuries, have a legend to explain how Chemainus got its name. There was a shaman named Tsa-meeun-is who somehow received a massive chest wound. When he recovered he became such a revered chief that his people named their community after him. (See the introduction to route 20 for more information on the town.)

Ladysmith's naming is a more prosaic story. The hillside town overlooking its eponymous harbour had its beginnings as a coal port built by the notorious coal baron James Dunsmuir. The workers in his mines south of Nanaimo needed to be housed, so Dunsmuir transformed the hillside behind the port into a small town for that purpose. In faraway South Africa, about the same time, the British Army were fighting their second war against the Boers. Being a proud Brit, Dunsmuir named the town in honour of the British victory over the Boers at the battle of Ladysmith. One thing you should know about the town, if you decide to explore it more fully, is that its hills are reminiscent of those of San Francisco, i.e., extremely steep. My "around town" route attempts to avoid the worst of them.

DISTANCE	27km/17mi.
LEVEL	Moderate.
HIGHLIGHTS	Murals in downtown Chemainus; stretches of seaside road; water and hillside views; downtown Ladysmith's early 20th century buildings; possible picnic at Ladysmith's Transfer Beach Park.
START	Chemainus Theatre at the corner of Chemainus Road and Victoria Street in downtown Chemainus.

The route

①　　　　　　　　　　　Leave from the front of the theatre and head north, i.e., toward Ladysmith on Chemainus Road.

②　(1.0km/0.6mi)　　At a roundabout, take the second R to continue on Chemainus Road.

③　(4.4km/2.7mi)　　Pass the junction with Old Victoria Road on the L. (You'll also come back on this road.)

④　(9.8km/6.1mi)　　The road swings L to join the Trans-Canada Highway. You turn R to ride on the highway's shoulder. (About 2km/1.2mi after this turn, on your R, is the entrance to Transfer Beach Park, a pleasant place to take a break.)

⑤　(12.9km/8.0mi)　　Here you have a decision to make. You can turn L at this traffic light at the north end of Ladysmith onto 1st Avenue (for cyclists, this is a tricky turn; in heavier traffic it might be better to walk across) and ride through Ladysmith's quaint downtown back to the highway and Chemainus Road at checkpoint 10, 3.4km/2.1mi away. Or you can follow my described route around the edge of town – a little longer route.

DOWNTOWN ROUTE:　　If you go through downtown, keep to 1st Avenue, which becomes Dogwood Drive, and descend to Davis Road. Turn L onto Davis and ride the short distance down to the Trans-Canada Highway to checkpoint 10.

CIRCLE ROUTE:　　Continue on the highway for a further 600m/yd and turn L onto Grouhel Road. (This is another tricky

Top: *Transfer Beach Park.*
Bottom: *Taking a break in downtown Ladysmith.*

turn in traffic. It might be safer to dismount and walk over to Grouhel Road.)

⑥ (13.7km/8.5mi) After 200 m/yd on Grouhel turn L onto Christie Road.

⑦ (14.2km/8.8mi) Turn L onto 4th Avenue and then R onto Walkem Road. Keep to Walkem as it becomes Colonia Drive (at Brown Road L). After almost a kilometre/600yards, turn L onto Malone Road.

⑧ (15.0km/9.3mi) Turn R onto 6th Avenue, and when 6th Avenue ends, turn L onto Methuen Street.

⑨ (15.7km/9.8mi) Just before Methuen's dead end, turn R onto Dogwood Drive. (1st Avenue goes L). Follow Dogwood on a long downhill to its junction with Davis Road and turn L down to the Trans-Canada Highway.

⑩ (18.1km/11.2mi) Cross the highway onto Chemainus Road, retracing the route until...

⑪ (23.4km/14.5mi) Watch for and take Old Victoria Road going R as Chemainus Road bears L.

⑫ (27.7km/17.2mi) At the roundabout turn R to join Chemainus Road to ride back to the route's start in Chemainus.

PART THREE: NANAIMO

At first glance, Nanaimo might not seem like the kind of city you'd want to ride in, through or around. But just scratch its surface and you'll discover some delightfully pleasant roads and places with intriguing names and histories.

The three rides described below all start at Nanaimo's oldest building, the Bastion. Built in 1853 by the Hudson's Bay Company, the octagonal structure was the company's fortification of its burgeoning area coal mines. For the time, effort and money spent on the building, there has never been a major attack on the structure or the city. The Bastion is now a city museum and sees far more use than as a fort. The one or two blocks west of the Bastion are part of Nanaimo's old town. Small stores and commercial buildings line narrow streets which have the occasional cobbled sections.

Behind the Bastion is the city's harbour, with an array of docks, small parks, stores, cafes and restaurants. And there's the Harbourfront Walkway, which, at its northern end, overlooks the small Newcastle Island. Although this is a multi-use path, I believe its best use is on foot.

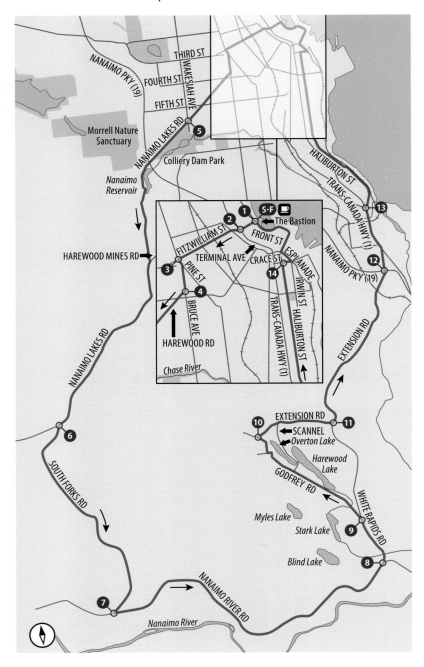

Nanaimo – Southwest Loop

This route, once you leave Nanaimo's streets, heads out of town and towards the Nanaimo River. But until the river, you'll pass through a quintessential BC working forest as you ride along Nanaimo Lakes and South Forks roads. There are cut blocks, log dump sites and row upon row of recently planted trees. Although the river is elusive, there's access to it at what is known locally as the Pink Rock access gate, about 3km/1.9mi past the South Forks Road junction (checkpoint 7) on Nanaimo River Road. Travelling north on White Rapids Road, the route detours towards the village of Extension, a now defunct mining community of the Wellington Colliery Company. (It was previously called Wellington Extension, Wellington being one of the company's main coal mines, 13km/8mi to the north.) Once over the Trans-Canada Highway, you enter Nanaimo on Haliburton Street, riding through one of the older parts of the city.

DISTANCE	32km/20mi.
LEVEL	Moderate.
HIGHLIGHTS	Riding some of the less frequented roads southwest of Nanaimo; river access; the old mining village of Extension.
START	The Bastion on Front Street, downtown Nanaimo.

The route

①		From the Bastion ride up Bastion Street to a set of traffic lights and continue straight as Bastion becomes Fitzwilliam Street.
②	(300m/yd)	Continue on Fitzwilliam Street.
③	(1.1km/0.7mi)	At the third set of lights turn L onto

Bruce Avenue. (Pine Street goes R at this intersection.)

④ (1.5km/0.9mi)   A short distance later turn R onto Harewood Road.

⑤ (2.6km/1.6mi)   After a number of four-way stops look for the four-way stop that crosses over onto Nanaimo Lakes Road. (Wakesiah Avenue is the cross street.) The entrance to Colliery Dam Park is on your L a short distance along Nanaimo Lakes Road.

⑥ (9.1km/5.6mi)   As the road bears L it becomes South Forks Road.

⑦ (13.1km/8.1mi)   Turn L onto Nanaimo River Road at the South Forks Road junction.

⑧ (19.0km/11.8mi)   Turn L at a wide junction onto White Rapids Road.

⑨ (20.0km/12.4mi)   As the road appears to fork, turn L onto Godfrey Road.

⑩ (22.4km/13.9mi)   Keep to Godfrey as it winds around the eastern edge of the small community of Extension. At a stop sign turn sharp R 180° onto Extension Road. (Going straight would take you into the small village itself, with its miniature park and covered bridge on the R.)

⑪ (23.9km/14.8mi)   Turn L at a stop sign. This is the junction with White Rapids Road, which now continues as Extension Road.

⑫ (27.4km/17.0mi)   Follow Extension under the highway bypass, and shortly after it becomes Cranberry Road, turn L onto the

The Bastion.

		wide shoulder of the Trans-Canada Highway.
⑬	(28.1km/17.5mi)	After passing under a railway bridge turn R onto Haliburton Street. (Haliburton is signed as a cycle route.)
⑭	(31.3km/19.4mi)	Haliburton ends at Crace Street. Turn R onto Crace, then L onto Esplanade, then R onto Front Street in quick succession. You now ride the 700m/yd back to the Bastion.

Opposite: *A remembrance of Chinese mine workers.*
Above: : *Mining history.*

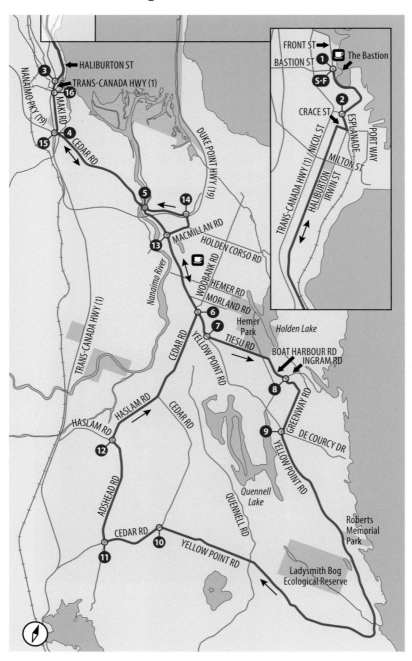

Nanaimo – Southeast Loop

A few kilometres southeast of downtown Nanaimo are lands that, for over a century, have provided food for Vancouver Island's inhabitants. Fifty years ago these lands and others like it on the Island provided islanders with 85 per cent of their food supply. Today, it's only a fraction of that: 10 per cent, to be exact. Despite this significant diminution, the countryside you'll ride through supports a surprising number of small- and medium-scale family-run farms that grow a variety of crops from hay and vegetables to berries and fruit trees. And, typical of farming communities, they also raise beef cattle, poultry and sheep. So it's not surprising that on this almost 50-km/30-mi jaunt, you'll ride amongst a smattering of well-cared-for farms with their attendant aromas, visual delights and roadside stands.

DISTANCE	48km/30mi.
LEVEL	Moderate.
HIGHLIGHTS	Two provincial parks: Hemer and Roberts Memorial; beach access; access road to Yellow Point Lodge; Cedar village; coffee shop; pub.
START	The Bastion on Front Street in downtown Nanaimo.

The route

①		From the Bastion ride south on Front Street toward the harbour. Keep on Front Street for about 700m/yd.
②	(700m/yd)	Turn L on Esplanade, then first R onto Crace Street and then L onto Haliburton Street. All of these are signed as cycle routes.
③	(3.9km/2.4mi)	Haliburton junctions the

Trans-Canada Highway. Cross (with care) and turn L onto the highway.

④ (5.3km/3.3mi) Having moved into the L turning lane, turn L onto Cedar Road. (This junction is partially under the overpass for the Nanaimo Parkway.)

⑤ (8.3km/5.1mi) Just over the Nanaimo River bridge, turn R onto a continuation of Cedar Road.

⑥ (11.3km/7.0mi) Having passed through the village of Cedar, you turn L onto Yellow Point Road.

⑦ (12.0km/7.5mi) Shortly after the turn onto Yellow Point Road, turn L again onto Tiesu Road (sign for both Tiesu and Boat Harbour roads). (If you feel like having a pint, there's a pub 1km/0.6mi away, off Yellow Point Road.) There are a couple of access trails into Hemer Provincial Park on your L along this road. Tiesu becomes Boat Harbour Road after 1.5km/1mi.

⑧ (14.3km/8.9mi) As the road bears L at Ingram Road, you turn R onto Greenway Road, a tree-lined stretch you'll be pleased to be riding.

⑨ (15.9km/9.9mi) Turn R onto Decourcy Drive, then immediately L onto Yellow Point Road.

⑩ (27.7km/17.2mi) This long stretch of road takes you past Roberts Memorial Provincial Park, Blue Heron Park (picnic area and easy beach access) and the access road to Yellow Point Lodge respectively. At the junction of Yellow

Top: *Bridge over the Nanaimo River.*
Bottom: *A tranquil pond along Tiesu Road.*

Point Road and Cedar Road, turn L onto Cedar Road.

⑪ (29.2km/18.1) Turn R onto Adshead Road just past the North Oyster Community Centre (L).

⑫ (31.9km/19.8mi) At a fork in the road take the R fork onto Haslam Road. You now have a 6km/3.7mi jaunt back to Cedar village. As Haslam joins Cedar Road bear L. As Yellow Point Road joins Cedar bear L.

⑬ (37.9km/23.5mi) Turn R onto Macmillan Road metres/yards past the hardware store (R).

⑭ (38.8km/24.1mi) After the road overpasses the Duke Point Highway turn L onto Harmac Road.

⑮ (42.8km/26.6mi) Harmac Road becomes Cedar Road just before the Nanaimo River bridge. As Cedar Road intersects the Trans-Canada Highway turn R.

⑯ (43.9km/27.3mi) Ride through the Maki Road/10th Street junction and take the first road on your R. This is Haliburton Street. You now retrace the route back along Haliburton to Front Street and the Bastion, almost 4km/2.5mi away.

This delightful little park even has a beach.

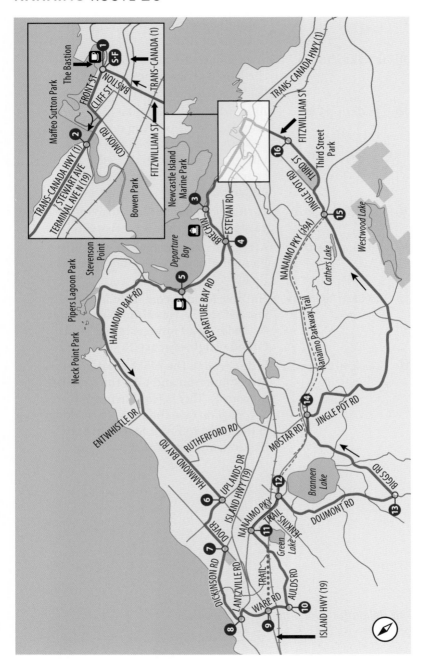

Nanaimo – North Loop

Of all the road names in and around Nanaimo, none arouses curiosity as much as Jingle Pot Road. Where did such a name come from? Well, it's a coal-mining term. For many years, north Nanaimo was known as Wellington, a coal-mining town established by the coal baron Robert Dunsmuir back in the late 1800s. At the bottom of a mine shaft, when a full coal cart was ready to be hauled to the surface, the miner in charge would signal to the hoist operator at the top by pulling on a rope attached to a metal container (a pot) full of small stones. The sound, or "jingle," the pot made was the signal to begin the hoist. The road's name is a rather poetic reminder of Nanaimo's industrial and grimier past.

DISTANCE	44km/27mi.
LEVEL	Moderate to strenuous.
HIGHLIGHTS	Departure Bay Park; Pipers Lagoon and Neck Point parks; Westwood Lake Park; country roads west of the city, including Jingle Pot Road.
START	The Bastion on Front Street in downtown Nanaimo.

The route

①		From the Bastion ride north on Front Street in the direction of the ferry terminal. After turning sharp L onto Comox Road, turn R onto the Trans-Canada Highway.
②	(900m/yd)	Bear R onto the Trans-Canada as it heads toward the Departure Bay ferry terminal. This is known locally as Stewart Avenue but is also signed for Highway 1 and Vancouver.
③	(3.0km/1.9mi)	At the traffic lights to the entrance

of the ferry terminal, turn L onto the rising Brechin Road. (This is signed for Parksville.)

④ (4.0km/2.5mi) Turn R at the traffic lights onto Estevan Road, and after 100m/yd turn R again onto Departure Bay Road. You now descend to Departure Bay itself, with its shoreline park.

⑤ (6.1km/3.8mi) As the road bears L and rises from the bay, turn sharply R onto Hammond Bay Road, a long ascent. Look for Pipers Lagoon and Neck Point parks on your R a few kilometres/miles along Hammond Bay Road – both very pleasant resting spots.

⑥ (15.6km/9.7mi) At the third set of lights turn R onto Uplands Drive. After a further 1.5km/0.9mi turn L at a four-way stop onto Dover Road.

⑦ (17.9km/11.1mi) At the next light turn R onto Dickinson Road.

⑧ (20.1km/12.5mi) As Dickinson intersects Lantzville Road at Lantzville's village centre, you turn L. There are a few amenities here, including a pub. After 300 metres/yards, turn R off Lantzville Road onto Ware Road.

⑨ (21.2km/13.2mi) Cross the Island Highway (19) at the lights to continue on Ware.

⑩ (21.8km/13.5mi) Not long after crossing the highway, turn sharp L onto Aulds Road. (For those wanting a break from the road, there's an alternative route to the next checkpoint using a paved trail that starts 200m/yd from the

Almost multi-use!

highway, on the L just before the railway tracks crossing Ware Road. The trail ends at Clark Drive where Clark junctions Aulds Road. To join this route, turn R off the trail and then L onto Aulds.)

⑪ (24.4km/15.2mi) As Aulds Road joins the Nanaimo Parkway take the R access lane, and just before you come to the parkway itself, turn R onto the paved Parkway Trail. Although this is a well-maintained trail, it's not exactly flat and uses roadway some of the time. It parallels Jenkins Road for a while.

⑫ (25.6km/15.9mi) At the crosswalk at the end of Jenkins, turn R onto Doumont Road. Now starts a longish stretch of country road. Views over Brannen Lake are on your L.

⑬ (29.1km/18.1mi) As Doumont joins Biggs Road, turn L onto Biggs. (Pay no attention to the correctional centre on your R.)

⑭ (32.5km/20.2mi) At a stop sign, turn R onto Jingle Pot Road. In the distance, Mt. Benson rises to your R. Shortly before Jingle Pot's junction with the Nanaimo Parkway, the access road to Westwood Lake Park – Westwood Road – is on the R. There are now views of the city, the ocean and the Coast Mountains.

⑮ (40.3km/25.0mi) Cross the Nanaimo Parkway, keeping to Jingle Pot Road. As Jingle Pot goes L you continue straight as the road now becomes Third Street. Keep to Third Street as it morphs into Fitzwilliam Street on the edge of downtown. (You pass an aquatic centre (R) and an ice rink (L) on your descent into town.)

(16) (43.4km/27mi) In downtown Nanaimo, Fitzwilliam becomes Bastion Street. Follow Bastion for a few hundred metres/yards to its end at Front Street and the Bastion.

Neck Point Park.

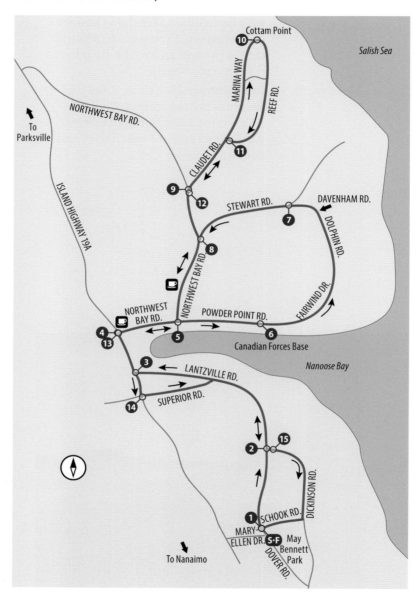

Lantzville – Nanoose Bay Loop

Lantzville, named after an American coal mine investor, Fraser Harry Lantz, is a small coastal community just north of Nanaimo. Coal was discovered and mined in the early years of the twentieth century. As the seams ran out the place morphed into a pleasant rural sibling of its much larger sister, Nanaimo. It has a small grocery store and a village pub.

Nanoose Bay lies just north of Lantzville and is, essentially, a large rural enclave. It's well known for its golf course, marina and yacht club. It's also home to the Canadian Forces Maritime Experimental Test Range, a joint Canadian and American facility. Its name is an anglicized form of the First Nation (Snaw-Naw-As) who live in the area.

This ride, although starting in Nanaimo, takes you onto two peninsulas – one large, the other smaller – that jut into the Salish Sea just north of the city. Apart from local traffic, the roads are not crowded, and though not endowed with marked shoulders, they're safe enough.

DISTANCE	47km/29mi.
LEVEL	Moderate to strenuous.
HIGHLIGHTS	Pleasant paved roads that circumnavigate two peninsulas; beach accesses; regional parks; possible stop at the Lantzville pub before the ride's end.
START	Parking area of May Bennett Park on Dover Road (opposite Mary Ellen Drive) in Nanaimo.

The route

①		From the parking area ride north on Dover Road toward Lantzville. Dover Road soon becomes Lantzville Road.
②	(2.0km/1.2mi)	Pass through Lantzville's small downtown.

③ (5.7km/3.5mi) Turn R onto Highway 19. There's a wide shoulder all the way to the next checkpoint. You soon notice the wide bay on your R with the rising headland of Powder Point.

④ (11.8km/7.3mi) At a major traffic-lighted intersection, turn R onto Northwest Bay Road.

⑤ (13.0km/8.1mi) After crossing the railway lines, turn R onto Powder Point Road. (A small mall with grocery store and café are 100m/yd or so on the L off Northwest Bay Road.) This road takes you past the Canadian Forces Maritime Experimental and Test Ranges and into the peninsula's housing, golf and marina community.

⑥ (16.8km/10.4mi) As Powder Point Road turns sharply R onto the Canadian Forces base, you continue straight on the windy and hilly Fairwinds Drive.

⑦ (18.7km/11.6mi) With Fairwinds Golf Club on your R, the road swings L to become Dolphin Drive. Dolphin eventually becomes Davenham Road after about 5km/3mi) and then, at a bend L, becomes Stewart Road (which comes in from the R and leads to Moorecroft Regional Park).

⑧ (25.4km/15.8mi) At a stop sign, turn R onto Northwest Bay Road. (For a slightly shorter ride (by 6km/3.7mi), turn L onto Northwest Bay Road and ride it back to checkpoint 13.)

⑨ (25.8km/16mi) After 400m/yd you turn R onto Claudet Road, which leads you to a very pleasant loop around Cottam

Top: *Notch Hill overlooking Nanoose Bay.*
Bottom: *Schooner Cove marina.*

Point. Continue on Claudet Road for 1.7km/1.0mi and bear L as the road becomes Marina Way (Dorcas Point Road goes R). You pass Beachcomber Regional Park on your L and, as Marina swings R, Seadog Road, also on your L. Cottam Point, at the end of this very short road, is well known as a scuba-diving beach.

⑩ (29.5km/18.3mi)   After Seadog, continue on Marina Way, which soon becomes Reef Road as Marina swings R.

⑪ (31.0km/19.3mi)   At Reef Road's later junction with Marina Way, turn L onto Marina and ride 700m/yd to where it becomes Claudet Road at the Dorcas Point Road junction, bearing R onto Claudet.

⑫ (31.7km/19.7mi)   Turn L onto Northwest Bay Road. Follow the road to its junction with Highway 19. You will have passed the small mall on your R 1.5km/1mi before the junction. (For a longer ride, by 14km/8.7mi, turn R onto Northwest Bay Road and ride just over 6km/3.7mi to the outskirts of Parksville. As Northwest Bay Road joins Highway 19A turn L and follow the highway in the direction of Nanaimo to Nanoose. Pass the Nanoose junction and join the route at checkpoint 14.)

⑬ (35.0km/21.7mi)   Turn L onto the highway. You're now retracing the route back to Dover Road.

⑭ (40.0km/24.8mi)   At the first traffic light, turn L onto

Lantzville Road. (A gas station is at this junction.)

⑮ (45.5km/28.3mi)   In Lantzville, turn L opposite the pub onto Dickinson Road. After 1.5km/1mi watch for and turn R onto Schook Road. Turn L at the top of the 500m/yd Schook Road hill onto Dover Road and the ride's start.

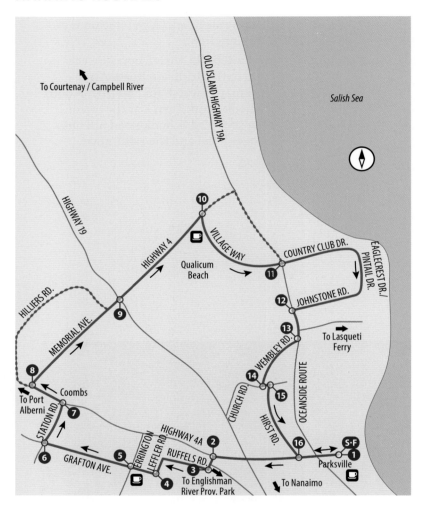

Parksville / Errington / Coombs / Qualicum Beach Loop

The Parksville area has been settled for eons by Coast Salish First Nations. But, not surprisingly, the British explorer Captain George Vancouver was the first European to visit, around 1792. (Although the Spanish had been sniffing around at about the same time, as the early names of the Englishman River and French Creek attest: Rio de Grullas (River of Cranes) and Punta de Leonardo.)

It wasn't until the 1880s that permanent settlers began to put down stakes. In fact, the city's name is derived from one of those early settlers, Nelson Parks. He opened a post office in 1886 and became the first postmaster. Over the years, his surname evolved into the longer (and fancier) Parksville.

DISTANCE	36km/22mi.
LEVEL	Moderate.
HIGHLIGHTS	The village of Coombs and its famous market (with goats on its roof); possible visit to Englishman River Provincial Park; Qualicum Beach township; Qualicum Beach's beach; coffee stops in Errington, Coombs and Qualicum Beach.
START	Parking area of Parksville's waterfront Community Park.

The route

①   Exit the park on the one-way Beachside Drive to the highway and turn R. Ride to the traffic lights and turn L onto the Alberni Highway. This takes all of 400m/yd.

② (3.1km/1.9mi)   After leaving the town behind, keep to the Alberni Highway as you negotiate a large cloverleaf intersection. Almost immediately (600m/yd) after passing under the overpass turn L onto Bellevue Road.

③ (4.6km/2.8mi)   Bear sharply R onto Ruffels Road as Bellevue goes straight.

④ (6.2km/3.8mi)   Ruffels turns L to become Leffler Road. After 1km/0.6mi turn R onto Grafton Avenue at the stop sign.

⑤ (8.0km/5mi)   Pass through the village of Errington. To the L is the way to Englishman River Falls Provincial Park, 7km/4.3mi away at the end of Errington Road.

⑥ (11.5km/7.1mi)   Turn R off Grafton onto Station Road.

⑦ (13.2km/8.2mi)   At a stop sign turn L onto the Alberni Highway. The famous Old Country Market in the village of Coombs is on your L about 400m/yd up the road.

⑧ (16.0km/9.9mi)   At the major intersection, turn R onto Highway 4 (aka Memorial Avenue). Highways 4 and 4A merge at this point going west. (For a 5km/3mi longer (and quieter) ride, turn L onto Highway 4 and ride 1.6km/1mi to turn R onto Hilliers Road South. Follow Hilliers to its junction with Highway 4 and turn L, a 4.5km/2.8mi ride. You're now on your way to checkpoint 9.)

⑨ (18.6km/11.5mi)   Pass under Highway 19.

⑩ (21.4km/13.3mi)   Having ridden through downtown Qualicum Beach and as the road starts to descend, turn R onto the wide Village Way. (If you prefer to see the water again, continue down the hill to Highway 19A, aka Island Highway and Oceanside Route, and turn R, rejoining the route at checkpoint 11.)

⑪ (24.2km/15.0mi) At Village Way's junction with Highway 19A, cross over and take Country Club Drive (and enter golf land!). You now cycle a 3.5km/2.2mi semi-circle to join Highway 19A. So... at the end of Country Club Drive turn R onto Eaglecrest Drive. As Eaglecrest turns abruptly R at a four-way stop sign, you continue straight on Pintail Drive. Cross Yambury Road (another four-way stop), and at the next stop sign turn R onto Johnstone Road.

⑫ (27.7km/17.8mi) Turn L onto Highway 19A.

⑬ (29.3km/18.2mi) Just after the Lasqueti Island Ferry/ Lee Road intersection, bear R onto Wembley Road. Keep to Wembley until a three-way stop (behind a shopping mall).

⑭ (31.5km/19.6mi) Turn R onto Church Road and then, at a roundabout, turn R at the third exit, onto Humphrey Road. Two hundred metres/yards on Humphrey turn R onto Renz Road.

⑮ (33.0km/20.5mi) Renz Road turns sharply L to become Hirst Avenue.

⑯ (35.2km/21.9mi) In downtown Parksville, turn L onto the Alberni Highway and ride the two blocks to Highway 19A. At the highway turn R, and 500m/yd later turn L at a traffic light onto Corfield Street to ride back into the park.

North Island
Wildlife
Recovery
Centre

Public Viewing

WILDLIFE GARDEN
GIFT SHOP

VANCOUVER ISLAND
Black Bear
Rehabilitation
Facility

OPEN
9:00 AM - 4:30 PM

1240

Opposite: *The Wildlife Recovery Centre at Errington.*
Above: *Inside the Old Country Market in Coombs.*

PART FOUR:
PORT ALBERNI

The Alberni Inlet is the longest on Vancouver Island and Port Alberni sits at its head. It was an ideal place for enterprising colonists to start a sawmill, being surrounded by an abundance of forest and easy access to tidewater. That was in 1861, the same year credited with the beginning of the town's colonial settlement. Since that time, there have been a number of mills – sawmills and pulp mills – that have come and gone. Nonetheless, the lumber industry has remained central to the town's economy, and the town's historical past is now part of its thriving tourism sector.

Of course, Indigenous people had inhabited the area for eons before the Europeans arrived. They knew the importance of the place's geography to their way of life and culture. The Tseshaht and the Hupačasath are the largest First Nations living in the area and are part of the much larger Nuu-chah-nulth Tribal Council. The Tseshaht have a magnificent administration building on the west side of town, off Highway 4. The Ahtsik Native Art Gallery is a further 2km/1.2mi away, also off Highway 4.

The town is bifurcated by the two highways leading into it, and the majority of its "downtown" is situated on the town's south side. The shorter of the three rides described below explores some of this pleasant part of town.

The two major events in the town's recent history are the 7.5 magnitude earthquake that occurred in 1946 and the two 1964 tsunamis that hit the west coast of British Columbia. The latter caused considerable destruction, with almost 400 of the town's homes damaged and 55 washed away. Though the physical scars of the two catastrophes are gone, many of the older residents still have vivid memories of them both.

I wish I could say the waters of the inlet and the estuary of the Somass River (which drains into it) dominate the city from an aesthetic, touristic and cycling perspective, but they don't. Industry does. Apart from Victoria Quay and to a lesser extent Harbour Quay, the waters of the inlet are mostly hidden from view. Still, there's much to appreciate about the town and, farther afield, its rural landscape.

albernivalleytourism.com

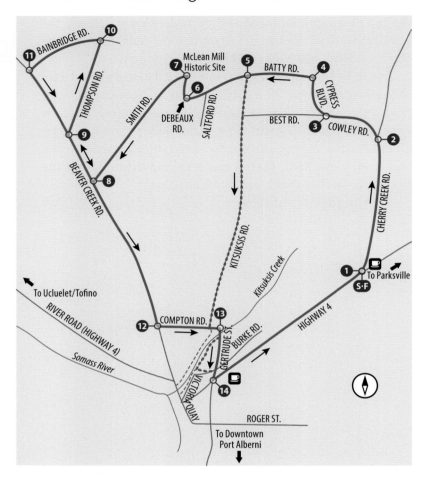

Port Alberni – Cherry Creek / Beaver Creek Loop

DISTANCE	24km/15mi.
LEVEL	Easy to moderate.
HIGHLIGHTS	McLean Mill National Historic Site; treed roadways; farmland; rural homesteads; possible visit to Stamp River Provincial Park; two alternative routes.
START	Parking area of the Pacific Rim Shopping Centre on the north side of Highway 4 at Cherry Creek Road.

The route

①   Exit the parking area and turn R onto the highway, then R onto Cherry Creek Road. (You can enter the parking area from Cherry Creek Road but you must exit on Highway 4.)

② (2.0km/1.2mi)   Opposite a church, turn L onto Cowley Road.

③ (3.0km/1.6mi)   Follow Cowley as it bends sharply R to become Cypress Boulevard. (Best Road continues straight.)

④ (4.5km/2.8mi)   to become Batty Road.

⑤ (5.6km/3.5mi)   Pass Kitsuksis Road on your L. (For a shorter route by 4km/2.5mi, turn L onto Kitsuksis and follow it to Compton Road. Turn L onto Compton and ride the short distance to checkpoint 13.)

⑥ (6.6km/4.1mi)   At an abrupt R turn, Batty becomes Debeaux Road.

⑦ (7.7km/4.8mi)   As Debeaux bears L at the entrance to the McLean Mill National Historic Site it becomes Smith Road.

⑧ (10.5km/6.5mi)   Turn R at the stop sign onto Beaver Creek Road.

⑨ (11.4km/7.1mi)   After a short distance take the second road on the R. This is Thompson Road. (You are now on a small triangle of roads that, if you're so inclined, you can ignore and head back on Beaver Creek Road to checkpoint 12.)

⑩ (13.2km/8.2mi)   As Thompson intersects Bainbridge Road, you turn L.

⑪ (14.7km/9.1mi)   At a stop sign, turn L back onto Beaver Creek Road. (To turn R here would take you to the entrance to Stamp River Provincial Park, 4km/2.5mi away.)

⑫ (19.8km/12.3mi)   Less than 400m/yd past an RV dealership on your R, look for and take Compton Road on your L.

⑬ (20.8km/12.9mi)   As the road bears R Compton morphs into Gertrude Street (Compton goes L). Continue on Gertrude. (To take the pleasant Kitsuksis Dyke Trail to the next checkpoint (14), turn R onto the paved path just past the bridge on Gertrude. Follow this creekside trail to its end at Victoria Quay. Turn L here and ride one-and-a-half blocks along Burke Road to Gertrude Street and turn R onto Gertrude. Checkpoint 14 is at the end of the street.)

⑭ (22.0km/13.7mi)   Turn L onto Johnston Road (aka Highway 4) and travel the almost 2km/1.3mi back to the ride's start at the Pacific Rim Shopping Centre.

To make this ride longer and incorporate the south side of the town, i.e., route #30, cross Johnston Road at checkpoint 14 onto the continuation of Gertrude Street to Pemberton Road and start the South Loop route from there. It will give you a total distance of about 36km/22mi.

Top: *The McLean Mill National Historic Site recounts Port Alberni's early days.*
Bottom: *Kitsuksis Creek Trail.*

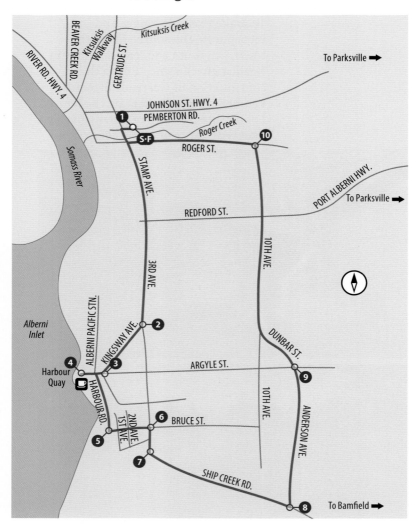

Port Alberni – South Loop

DISTANCE	12km/7.5mi.
LEVEL	Moderate to strenuous.
HIGHLIGHTS	Harbour Quay; Alberni Pacific Railway train station (possible train ride to McLean Mill Historic Park); Port Alberni Maritime Discovery Centre; edge of town neighbourhoods.
START	Parking area of Roger Creek Park at the corner of Gertrude Street and Pemberton Road.

The route

① From Pemberton Road turn L onto Gertrude Street. Gertrude soon becomes Stamp Avenue. At Redford Street, Stamp becomes 3rd Avenue.

② (2.1km/1.3mi) Just before a rise take the R exit onto Kingsway Avenue.

③ (2.4km/1.2mi) At Kingsway's junction with Argyle Street, turn R onto Argyle and ride the two blocks down to Harbour Quay. (The Alberni Pacific Railway train station is on your R on Harbour Road.)

④ (2.8km/1.7mi) Return from the Quay and turn R at the first intersection onto Harbour Road.

⑤ (3.8km/2.4mi) You soon pass the Port Alberni Maritime Discovery Centre on your R. Harbour Road effectively ends after about 1km/0.6mi at its junction with Bruce Street. Turn L onto Bruce.

⑥ (4.1km/2.5mi) At the top of two short hills turn R onto the wide 3rd Avenue.

⑦ (4.5km/2.8mi) Look for a road sign for Bamfield and

China Creek on the L. This is Ship Creek Road. Take it.

⑧ (5.9km/3.7mi)   The first major road on your L is Anderson Avenue. You turn onto it here. (After this point, Ship Creek Road becomes Franklin River Road, which meanders its way to Bamfield almost 90k/56mi away. Unfortunately, the road becomes gravel less than 5k/3mi from the Anderson Avenue junction.) The trailhead for the Alberni Inlet Trail is opposite this junction.

⑨ (8.1km/5.0mi)   Anderson crosses Argyle Street at a stop sign and becomes Dunbar Street. Continue on Dunbar for 350m/yd until it meets 10th Avenue. Turn R onto 10th Avenue.

⑩ (10.6km/6.6mi)   Keep to 10th Avenue as it crosses Redford Street (signed for Highway 4 east and west). On your R, four blocks past Redford, on Wallace Street, is the Alberni Valley Museum. At the next set of traffic lights, turn L onto Roger Street (also signed for Highway 4).

⑪ (11.6km/7.2mi)   After crossing railway lines, turn R at the traffic lights onto Gertrude Street and ride back to Pemberton Road and the start of the route.

Art as history at Victoria Quay.

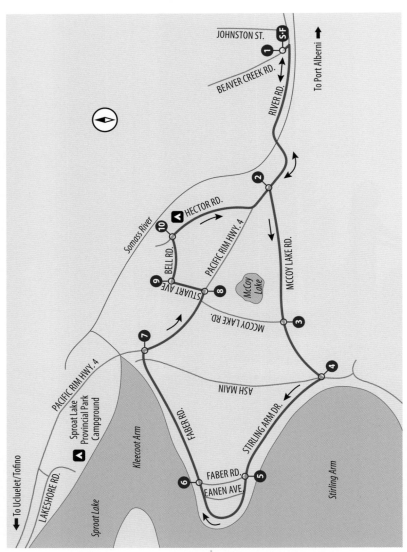

Port Alberni –
McCoy Lake Loop

DISTANCE	26km/16mi.
LEVEL	Moderate to strenuous.
HIGHLIGHTS	Farmland; lakeside homes; quiet country roads; possible visits to a riverside park and a First Nation art gallery.
START	Parking lot on Beaver Creek Road at its junction with Highway 4.

The route

① Leave the parking lot and turn L onto Beaver Creek Road then R onto Highway 4 (aka Pacific Rim Highway). As you'll be on this relatively busy road for a total of almost 8km/5mi, be extra mindful of the traffic.

View from Stirling Arm Road.

② (3.3km/2.0mi)   After crossing the Orange Bridge over the Somass River and just before the McCoy Creek bridge, turn L onto the hilly McCoy Lake Road. This can be a tricky turn if the traffic is heavy.

③ (6.3km/3.9mi)   At a sharp right-hand bend turn abruptly L onto Stirling Arm Drive. McCoy goes off to the R, which is now a private road and gated.

④ (8.1km/5.0mi)   Cross Ash Main Road.

⑤ (11.5km/7.1mi)   Pass Faber Road on your R. Stirling Arm Drive now becomes Stirling Arm Crescent.

⑥ (13.5km/8.4mi)   Having ridden around Stirling Head on Stirling Arm Crescent, you now join Faber Road at a stop sign as it comes in from your R.

⑦ (17.9km/11.1mi)   Faber joins Highway 4 at a stop sign. Turn R onto the highway.

⑧ (19.2km/11.9mi)   At a row of mail boxes on the L, turn L onto Stuart Avenue. (For a direct route back to the start or to visit the Ahtsik Native Art Gallery, continue on Highway 4. The gallery is a kilometre/0.6mi from here.)

⑨ (19.5km/ 12.1mi)   After a short way on Stuart turn R onto Bell Road.

⑩ (21.2km/13.2mi)   Turn R onto Hector Road at the stop sign. The entrance to Arrowvale Campground is immediately opposite. (The riverside Somass Park is about a kilometre/0.6mi to the L off Hector Road.)

Bell Road in the fall.

⑪ (23.0km/14.3mi)   As Hector ends, turn L onto Highway 4. You now ride the almost 4km/2.5mi back to the ride's start on Beaver Creek Road.

Kleecoot Arm of Sproat Lake.

PART FIVE:
COMOX VALLEY

No matter what the season, visiting the Comox Valley is a treat. In winter there's skiing – both cross-country and down-hill – and snowshoeing on Mt. Washington and in Strathcona Provincial Park. In spring, summer and fall there's walking, hiking, kayaking and, of course, cycling. Apart from the route up to Mt. Washington's ski resort, the following three routes are relatively flat and give a good sampling of why this area is one of the most desired places on the Island to live and visit.

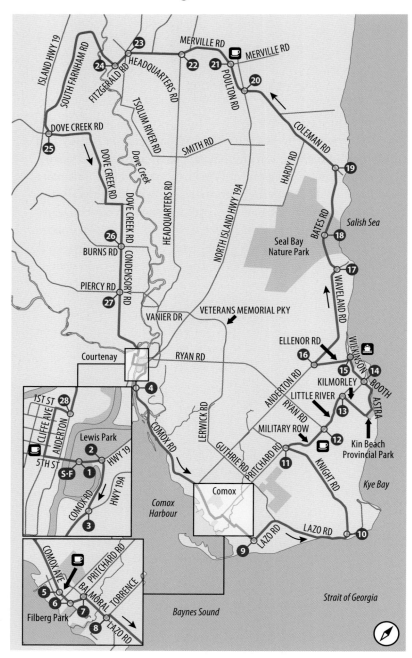

Tour of the Comox Valley

This ride is intended to skirt the region's two main towns, Courtenay and Comox, to take you close to nearby beaches and introduce you to the distinctive rural nature of the valley. Of course, you're never far from mountain views, of the Island's own peaks (including the Comox Glacier) as well as those of the Coast Mountains across the Salish Sea. You'll ride through the largest park in the valley, Seal Bay Nature Park. There are bike racks for your use if you decide to explore some of the park's trails. (For more details on the Comox Valley see my introduction to Stage 2 of ride 43 Victoria to Port Hardy, on page 261.)

DISTANCE	58km/36mi.
LEVEL	Easy to moderate.
HIGHLIGHTS	Town of Comox and its marina; views south from Point Holmes; CFB Comox; Kin Beach Provincial Park; Seal Bay Nature Park; country roads; farmland.
START	Simms Millennium Park, 5th Street opposite Lewis Park, downtown Courtenay.

The route

①		Leave the park by turning R onto 5th Street going northeast.
②	(100m/yd)	At the first traffic light turn R onto Comox Road.
③	(400m/yd)	Turn R again onto Comox Road/ Highway 19A.
④	(1.0km/0.6mi)	Continue straight over the junction with the 17th Street Bridge, keeping to Comox Road (locally known as the Dyke Road).
⑤	(6.0km/3.7mi)	Pass through Comox town centre. The

town's marina and park are down to your R.

(6) (6.5km/4.0mi) Bear L onto Pritchard Road.

(7) (6.9km/4.3mi) Turn R onto Balmoral Avenue.

(8) (7.5km/4.6mi) Turn L onto Torrence Road and then make a quick R onto Lazo Road. (To go straight from Balmoral on the dead-end Hawkins Road takes you to Goose Spit Park – a pleasant diversion.)

(9) (8.4km/5.2mi) Turn sharp L to follow the continuation of Lazo Road. This road leads to Point Holmes, a lovely beach area with views south over Denman and Hornby islands, the Beaufort Mountains and Mt. Arrowsmith in the distance (not to mention the Sunshine Coast, Texada Island and the Coast Mountains to the east).

(10) (12.0km/7.5mi) After passing Point Holmes, the road bears abruptly L (on a steep rise) to become Knight Road. The road is now bordered by CFB Comox's air base on the R side. The Comox Valley airport is on the R almost at the end of Knight Road.

(11) (16.0km/10mi) At the roundabout turn R onto Military Row. (You can guess where you are now.) Look for an impressive collection of military aircraft on the R side of the road.

(12) (17.6km/11.0mi) At the stop sign, go straight, crossing Ryan Road on what now becomes Little River Road.

(13) (19.0km/11.8mi) At the Griffin Pub sign on R, turn R onto Kilmorley Road. Then, after

about a kilometre (0.6mi), bear L onto Astra Road (signed for Kin Beach). The entrance to Kin Beach Provincial Park is on your R.

⑭ (21.0km/13.0mi)   Shortly after Astra bends L and becomes Booth Road turn R onto Little River Road and immediately go sharply L onto Wilkinson Road.

⑮ (22.6km/14.0mi)   Turn L onto Ellenor Road. To the R is the entrance to the Comox–Powell River ferry terminal.

⑯ (24.0km/15.0mi)   Turn sharply R onto the partly concealed Anderton Road. (Continuing straight would take you to Comox and Courtenay.) After about a kilometre/0.6mi and at a L bend, Anderton becomes Waveland Road.

⑰ (27.7km.17.2mi)   At a very tricky bend turn L onto Bates Road. (Signed for Campbell River via Highway 19A.)

⑱ (28.5km/17.7mi)   Boundary of Seal Bay Nature Park. A very pleasant 10 to 15 minute walk to park's beach on your R.

⑲ (31.5km/19.6mi)   At a stop sign turn L onto Coleman Road.

⑳ (35.7km/22.2mi)   Junction with Highway 19A. Cross the highway onto the narrow Poulton Road.

㉑ (37.0km/23.0mi)   At a stop sign, turn L onto Merville Road. If you're feeling peckish, though, you could take a brief detour R onto Merville and ride about 300m/yd to the stop sign at Highway 19A, where there's a small general store.

㉒ (38.9km/24.2mi)   Continue straight as Merville becomes Headquarters Road. (Headquarters also goes at a right angle to the L. This is an escape route back to Courtenay, 12km/6mi away.)

㉓ (40.6km/25.2mi)   Where Headquarters Road forks at a stop sign, turn L onto Fitzgerald Road.

㉔ (41.3km/25.7mi)   Turn R onto Farnham Road. This becomes South Farnham Road somewhere along its length before the next junction.

㉕ (47.0km/29.2mi)   As the road ends, turn L onto Dove Creek Road. To the R is Highway 19 and its junction with the Strathcona Parkway, the road up to Mt. Washington. (See route 35 on page 215)

㉖ (53.0km/33mi)   After two sweeping bends and at the junction of Dove Creek Road and Burns Road continue straight, on what is now Condensory Road.

㉗ (54.6km/34mi)   At a four-way junction with Piercy Road continue straight on Condensory.

㉘ (57.0km/35.1mi) Just over a wooden bridge turn R onto First Street, then L onto Cliffe Avenue, then L at the traffic lights onto Fifth Street and ride over the bridge back to Simms Park. (Sounds complicated but it's not.)

Opposite: *Riding across Goose Spit.*
Top: *View east from Point Holmes.*
Bottom: *Aviation history at CFB Comox.*

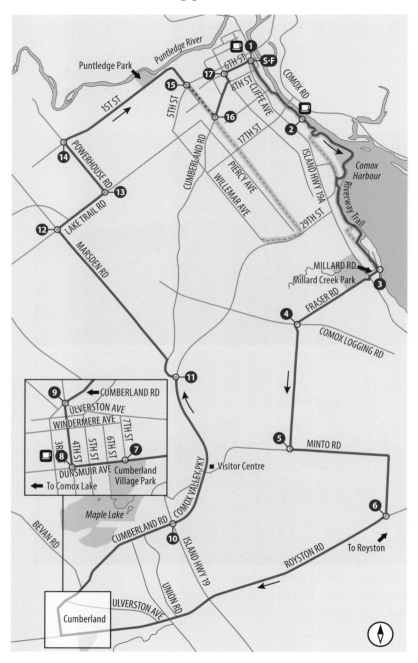

Courtenay Riverway Trail – Cumberland – Courtenay Loop

DISTANCE	26km/16mi.
LEVEL	Easy to moderate.
HIGHLIGHTS	Riverway trail; country roads; farmland; Cumberland township; suburban Courtenay; Rotary Trail.
START	Trailhead of the Courtenay Riverway trail on 6th Street, northeast of Cliffe Avenue.

The route

①   Take the multi-use paved trail heading south.

② (1.5km.1.0mi) Follow the trail keeping to the riverside as it passes a trailside café and skirts the local airstrip. The trail continues for some distance as pavement and then morphs into a good gravel pathway.

③ (3.5km/1.5mi) As the trail ends on Millard Road turn R and ride 50m/yd up to the intersection of Millard and Highway 19A. Turn L here and then R onto Fraser Road.

④ (4.7km/3.0mi) At the stop sign cross Comox Logging Road.

⑤ (6.5km/4.0mi) Turn L onto Minto Road at the stop sign. Keep to Minto as it turns sharply R.

⑥ (8.6km/5.3mi) Turn R onto Royston Road. After 2.5km/1.5mi you hit Boulder Hill, a rise that takes you over Highway 19.

⑦ (13.0km/8.1mi) The outskirts of Cumberland town centre.

⑧ (13.4km/8.3mi)   Turn R at a four-way stop onto Fourth Street.

⑨ (14.0km/8.7mi)   Bear R as Fourth Street becomes Cumberland Road.

⑩ (16.0km/10.0mi)   After passing under Highway 19 overpass, the road now becomes the Comox Valley Parkway. A short distance farther, on the R, is Minto Road, where an immediate additional R turn onto Small Road leads to the area's visitor centre in about 650m/0.4mi.

⑪ (18.2km/11.3mi)   At the traffic light turn L onto a continuation of Cumberland and then L again onto Marsden Road.

⑫ (20.8km/12.9mi)   Turn R onto Lake Trail Road at the stop sign.

⑬ (21.6km/13.2mi)   About 800m/yd along Lake Trail, turn L onto Powerhouse Road.

⑭ (22.5km/14mi)   At a four-way stop, turn R onto 1st Street. After a kilometre/0.6 mile you pass Puntledge Park on your L, along the banks of the Puntledge River.

⑮ (24.6km/15.3mi)   Shortly after climbing a steep hill along 1st Street that curves R and becomes Menzies Avenue, turn L onto 5th Street and then immediately R onto the 0.5km/0.3mi-long Rotary Trail that runs parallel to the railway.

⑯ (25.1km/15.6mi)   At the end of this short trail turn L onto Cumberland Road (yes, it's here again).

⑰ (25.7km/16mi)   Turn L at the traffic light onto Fitzgerald Avenue and ride to the next block to turn R onto 6th Street. At the bottom of 6th is the ride's start, less than 0.5km/0.3mi away.

Top: *Historic Cumberland.*
Bottom: *Checking out Courtenay's Riverway Trail*

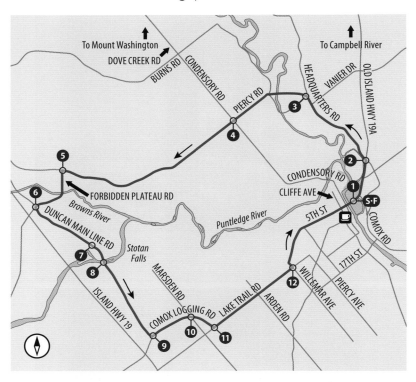

To Mount Washington
DOVE CREEK RD

To Campbell River

BURNS RD
CONDENSORY RD
PIERCY RD
HEADQUARTERS RD
VANIER DR
OLD ISLAND HWY 19A

3
4
5

CONDENSORY RD
FORBIDDEN PLATEAU RD
CLIFFE AVE
2
1
S·F
COMOX RD

6
Browns River
DUNCAN MAIN LINE RD
Puntledge River
5TH ST

7
Stotan
Falls
8

17TH ST
WILLEMAR AVE
PIERCY AVE

ISLAND HWY 19
MARSDEN RD
COMOX LOGGING RD
LAKE TRAIL RD
ARDEN RD
12

9
10
11

Courtenay West Loop (Headquarters / Piercy / Lake Trail)

DISTANCE	17km/11mi.
LEVEL	Easy.
HIGHLIGHTS	Country roads; farmland; Stotan Falls; downtown Courtenay.
START	Simms Millennium Park, 5th Street, opposite Lewis Park, downtown Courtenay.

The route

1. Exit the park by turning R onto 5th Street to head north out of town. This is the Old Island Highway to Campbell River.

2. (0.8km/0.4mi) At the third set of lights turn L onto Headquarters Road. The Island Highway, 19A, comes in from the R.

3. (2.5km/1.5mi) Bear L onto Piercy Road. (Headquarters goes to your R.)

4. (4.0km/2.5mi) Cross Condensory Road at a four-way stop.

5. (7.6km/4.7mi) Turn L onto Forbidden Plateau Road.

6. (8.6km/5.3mi) After crossing the Browns River bridge, turn L onto Duncan Bay Main Line Road. Ostensibly, this is a private road with a toll attached for vehicles. As of 2018, cyclists were no longer charged to travel the road.

7. (10.0km/6.2mi) Toll booth. No charge for cyclists.

8. (10.3km/6.4mi) Flat-deck bridge over the Puntledge River. Stotan Falls are on your L.

9. (12.2km/7.6mi) After riding through a gravelled

Top: *Stotan Falls.*
Bottom: *The Glacier.*

		lumber yard turn L onto the Comox Logging Road.
⑩	(13.0km/8.1mi)	Cross Marsden Road.
⑪	(13.5km/8.4mi)	Turn L onto Lake Trail Road.
⑫	(15.3km/9.5mi)	As Lake Trail ends turn L onto Willemar Avenue and then bear R as Willemar becomes 5th Street. Continue on 5th Street, passing through the centre of town and over the bridge back to Simms Park, a matter of just 2km/1.2mi.

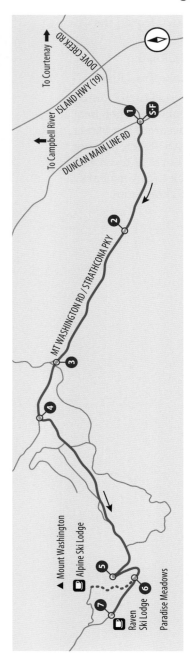

Strathcona Parkway to Paradise Meadows

The Strathcona Parkway is a popular road in both winter and summer. As its name suggests, it's a direct access to Strathcona Provincial Park and its Paradise Meadows. But the other reason it's there are the ski slopes of Mt. Washington, which, in the summer, become a mountain biker's heaven. The ride up the mountain is certainly a challenge and is not for those unwilling or unable to work hard. But like any challenge, there's a deal of satisfaction in accomplishing the top (not to mention the dramatic and spectacular views). Because the road is kept open year-round, it can be cycled year-round too!

DISTANCE	35km/22mi (out and back).
LEVEL	Strenuous.
HIGHLIGHTS	Grand views of the mountains of Strathcona Provincial Park; possible hike in the subalpine Paradise Meadows (or snowshoeing in winter); lunch at Raven Lodge or the Mt. Washington Alpine Lodge. Thrilling descent down the mountain.
START	Parking lot at the intersection of Strathcona Parkway and Duncan Bay Main Line Road.
HOW TO GET THERE	From downtown Courtenay ride across the 5th Street bridge to follow the Old Island Highway for a kilometre/0.6 mile and turn L at the traffic light onto Headquarters Road. At 2.7km/1.7mi turn L onto Piercy Road. Turn R onto Condensory Road at the four-way stop at 4.2km/2.6mi. Continue straight at the next stop sign as Condensory becomes Dove Creek Road. After 12.1km/7.5mi Dove Creek Road crosses the Island Highway to become Strathcona Parkway. If you're cycling, the ride is described from

the logging road a further 2km/1.2mi along the Parkway. If you're driving, there's ample parking at the ride's start.

The route

① From the parking lot turn R and cross Duncan Bay Main Line and begin the ride up the steep grade of the parkway. (This first, 3km/1.9ml pitch averages 12 per cent.)

② (4km/2.5mi) The road flattens for a few hundred metres. (Although the road to Paradise Meadows is a steady climb, it never becomes as steep as the first 3km/1.9mi.)

③ (6.2km/3.8ml) Pass the Anderson Hill chain-up area, a flattish section.

④ (10.6km/6.5mi) Pass the Ramparts Hill chain-up area, which is followed by a long downhill section.

⑤ (14km/8.7mi) With the Sunrise chair lift on your R, the road takes a rising 90° turn L.

⑥ (15.1km/9.4mi) Turn L onto Nordic Drive. (Strathcona Parkway continues for another kilometre or so (just over half a mile) to terminate at Mt. Washington's Alpine Lodge. This portion of road tips up at a grade of 12 per cent.)

⑦ (17.5km/10.9mi) The trailhead into Paradise Meadows is on your L. Raven Lodge is also here. Although the lodge primarily caters to winter sports, it is usually open year-round for refreshments.

The return ride can be very exhilarating. Be careful not to ruin your brake pads on the steeper parts of the descent.

PART SIX: CAMPBELL RIVER

Although Campbell River is a seaside town with its inevitable concentration of commercial and sport fishing enterprises, its close proximity to forest and mountains means that logging and outdoor pursuits are also part of its cultural and economic makeup.

The town itself has a very compact downtown with the small Robert V. Ostler Park next to a marina and the ferry terminal to Quadra and Cortes islands. One of the delights of the place is its Beaver Lodge Forest Lands, a 416-hectare piece of mostly rewilded parkland laced with hiking and biking trails. About 5km/3mi from downtown to the southwest, it's easily accessible. Though not described in this book, a map of the park trails is available at the town's visitor centre or on its website at campbellriver.travel.

To the west, along the highway to Gold River, are entrances to Elk Falls Provincial Park (not far from the town) and the northern wedge of Strathcona Provincial Park (about halfway to Gold River). Both are great places to hike and worth a detour if you're an avid hiker or curious or both.

Perhaps the most famous of Campbell River's former residents is Roderick Haig-Brown. A well-respected conservationist, author and judge, he lived just outside the town on the banks of the Campbell River from 1932 until his death in 1976. The family cottage is now a heritage site and open to the public – you and me!

The Quinsam River.

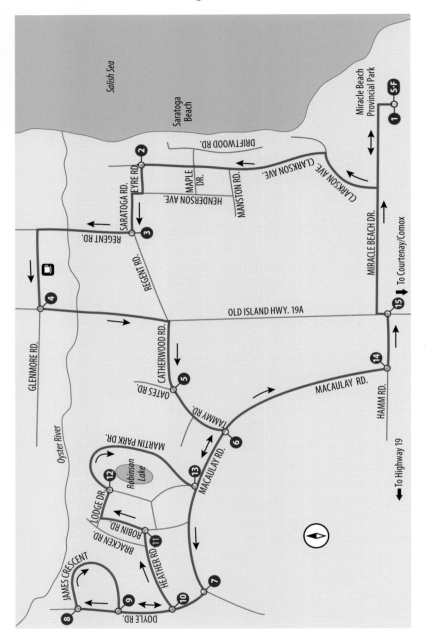

Oyster River / Miracle Beach

Roughly halfway between Courtenay and Campbell River, Oyster River is essentially a resort community that sustains a population of around 1,500 people. The river itself attracts fishers, kayakers, swimmers and the occasional gold prospector. It also has a sizable pink salmon run. West of Highway 19A there are a number of small residential enclaves, two of which are explored below.

DISTANCE	31km/19mi.
LEVEL	Easy to moderate.
HIGHLIGHTS	Access to beaches; parks large and small; quiet country roads.
START	Miracle Beach Provincial Park parking area.

The route

① From the parking area ride to the park entrance and turn R onto Clarkson Drive. Follow this road as it parallels the shores of Saratoga Beach. There are a number of beach accesses here, especially off Maple Drive and Driftwood and Seaman roads.

② (3.0km/1.9mi) Turn L onto Eyre Road at the No Thru Road sign. After one block, turn R onto Henderson Road, which becomes Saratoga Road at a sharp L turn.

③ (3.8km/2.4mi) Turn R onto Regent Road. You soon cross a girder bridge over the Oyster River, and after a 100m/yd or so, turn L onto Glenmore Road. (A grocery store and café is on your L along this short stretch of road.)

④ (4.4km/2.7mi)   At Glenmore's junction with Highway 19A, turn L onto the highway and ride 500m/yd to turn R onto Catherwood Road.

⑤ (6.0km/3.7mi)   At a stop sign, turn L onto Oakes Road. After 300m/yd turn L again onto Tammy Road.

⑥ (6.7km/4.2.7mi)   As Tammy Road ends, turn R onto a long section of Macaulay Road.

⑦ (13.2km/8.2mi)   Having passed Martin Park Drive and Robin Road on your R, turn R at the next R onto Doyle Road.

⑧ (15.0km/9.3mi)   Pass Heather Road on your R and Pinecrest and Dohm roads on your L (Pinecrest has an all-ages bike park). At a four-way junction, turn R onto James Crescent. (Islak Road goes L.) Continue on James Crescent as it "crescents" back to Doyle Road.

⑨ (16.1km/10.0mi)   Turn L back onto Doyle Road.

⑩ (17.6km/10.9mi)   Watch for and turn L onto Heather Road.

⑪ (19.0km/11.8mi)   Pass Bracken Road, which goes L and leads to Bracken Park, and as the road swings R, turn L onto Robin Road. Robin soon intersects Lodge Drive where you turn R onto Lodge.

⑫ (20.2km/12.5mi)   Turn L off Lodge onto Martin Park Drive. You now follow Martin Dark Drive as it circumnavigates Robinson Lake (which you can't see, unfortunately).

⑬ (21.3km/13.2mi)   At a stop sign, turn L onto a short

section of Martin Park Drive riding to its junction with Macaulay Road. Turn L onto Macaulay.

⑭ (28.0km/17.4mi)   Having just passed the entrance to the Saratoga Speedway (L) turn L at a stop sign onto Hamm Road.

⑮ (28.2km/17.5mi)   At the junction with the Island Highway (19A) turn L and then, 200m/yd later, turn R onto Miracle Beach Drive. You now ride the almost 3km/2mi back to the ride's start in the park.

Miracle Beach Park.

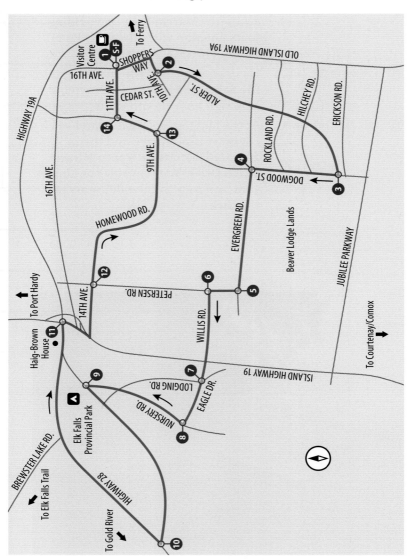

Tour of Campbell River

DISTANCE	38km/23.5mi.
LEVEL	Moderate to strenuous.
HIGHLIGHTS	The town's older and newer suburbs; views over Discovery Passage; farmlands; Beaver Lodge Forest Lands; fish hatchery; Elk Falls Provincial Park and the Roderick Haig-Brown Heritage House.
START	Campbell River visitor centre and mall parking area, Shoppers Row.

The route

①   From the parking area, exit at the "Logger Mike" pole, go directly across onto 10th Avenue and ride 100m/yd to turn L onto Alder Street. Ride a further 200m/yd and bear R as you cross St. Ann's Road to continue on Alder Street.

② (0.5km/0.3mi)   Bear R as Alder continues to climb from the town's centre. You stay on Alder for the next 7km/4.3mi. The road is a lumpy one and crosses a number of traffic-lighted and stop-signed junctions before it ends at South Dogwood Street.

③ (7.5km/4.7mi)   Turn R onto South Dogwood Street. There is a multi-use path running beside this wide road going north. It lasts for almost 5km/3mi before finishing at the junction with Robron Road. You'll notice also on this stretch the many access trails to the Beaver Lodge Lands on your L. This large, park-like parcel was given in trust to the people of Campbell River by a local timber company in the early

1930s. Although meant for forestry research, it is, de facto, an enchanting piece of reclaimed wild Earth that is open to the public, with many trails and natural features. Continue northward on Dogwood.

④ (13.8km/8.6mi) At a traffic-light junction turn L onto Evergreen Road.

⑤ (15.1km/9.4mi) At a four-way stop turn R onto Petersen Road.

⑥ (15.9km/9.9mi) Just before a pedestrian crossing turn L onto Willis Road.

⑦ (17.3km/10.7mi) After crossing the Inland Island Highway (19) and about 300m/yd farther, at a T intersection, bear R onto Eagle Drive.

⑧ (18.3km/11.4mi) At a three-way stop turn R onto Nursery Road. Continue on this road to its end.

⑨ (19.8km/12.3mi) Where Nursery ends turn L onto Quinsam Road. The entrance to the Quinsam River fish hatchery is about 2km/1.3mi on the L. Passing under a powerline, Quinsam becomes Argonaut Road.

⑩ (26.5km/16.5mi) As Argonaut Road meets the Gold River Highway (aka Highway 28) turn R onto the highway. After 3km/2mi or so, you pass through Elk Falls Provincial Park. This is a largish park with a number of access points.

⑪ (34.9km/21.7mi) Having just passed the Quinsam Road junction on your R and the Haig-Brown House on your L, turn R at a major, traffic-lighted intersection onto the one-way Willow Street, which is also the southbound part of Inland Island Highway (19), signed for Nanaimo. Five hundred metres/yards later, turn L onto 14th Avenue.

⑫ (36.2km/22.5mi)   14th Avenue swings R to become Homewood Road. After 1km/0.6mi Homewood becomes 9th Avenue.

⑬ (37.7km/23.2mi)   Turn L at the first major intersection, onto Dogwood Street. At the bottom of the short but steep Dogwood Street hill turn R onto 11th Avenue to travel the 300m/yd back to the ride's start at the visitor centre.

Campbell River's past?

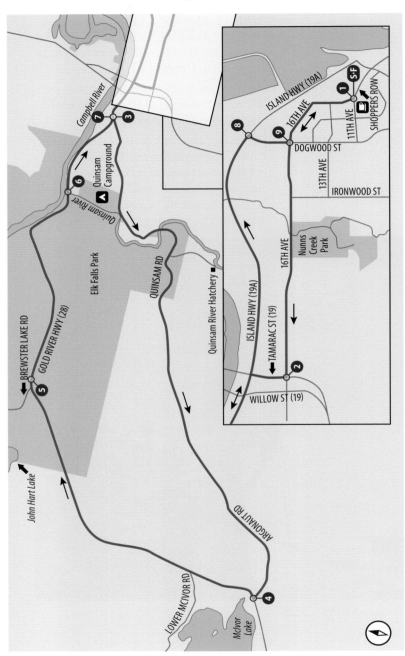

Campbell River West Loop

DISTANCE	21km/13mi.
LEVEL	Moderate.
HIGHLIGHTS	Elk Falls Provincial Park (trails, waterfalls, suspension bridge); Haig-Brown Heritage House; country roads; fish hatchery.
START	Campbell River visitor centre and mall parking area, Shoppers Row.

The route

(1) From the parking area turn R onto Shoppers Row, which quickly becomes 16th Avenue. Keep to 16th Avenue as it takes you to the edge of town.

(2) (2.2km/1.4mi) Turn R onto the one-way, traffic-lighted Tamarac Street. After 250m/yd, turn L onto Highway 19A, which, at the next set of lights becomes Highway 28 (aka Campbell River Road and Gold River Highway).

(3) (2.9km/1.8mi) After passing the Haig-Brown Heritage House (R) look for and turn L onto Quinsam Road. For the next few kilometres/miles you'll ride along an undulating rural road with open fields much of the way. You'll also pass the entrance to the Quinsam River fish hatchery about 2.5km/1.5mi on the L along this road.

(4) (10.1km/6.3mi) Quinsam Road (now named Argonaut Road) ends at its junction with Highway 28, the Gold River Highway. Turn R here. In less than a kilometre/

mile, on the L, is Lower McIvor Lake Road, the access to McIvor Lake, a pleasant picnic and swimming place. The road travels through an avenue of conifers and, not too far up the road, traverses Elk Falls Provincial Park.

(5) (13.0km/8.0mi)   At a long R bend, on your L, is Brewster Lake Road, a main entrance to Elk Falls park and the closest parking area to the falls' suspension bridge. Another access to the park is John Hart Road, also on the L, a little farther along.

(6) (15.7km/9.7mi)   After a long, steep downhill, on the R, is the entrance to the park's Quinsam Campground. Set on the high banks of the Quinsam River, it's an attractive, spacious facility. Across the highway and slightly to the R are two park entrances. The one over the Campbell River itself gives access to the river's Canyon View Trail.

(7) (17.0km/10.5mi)   Pass Quinsam Road on the R and the Haig-Brown house on the L. Keep to the highway, resisting any turn R until...

(8) (19.4km/12.0mi)   ... after a long, sweeping right-hand bend, where, at a major traffic-light intersection, you turn R onto the well-signed Dogwood Street. Ride to the next lighted intersection.

(8) (20.0km/12.4mi)   Turn L onto 16th Avenue. Keep to 16th for about 400m/yd back to the ride's start at the visitor centre.

Top: *Elk Falls/Quinsam campground.*
Bottom: *Checking on the spawning salmon.*

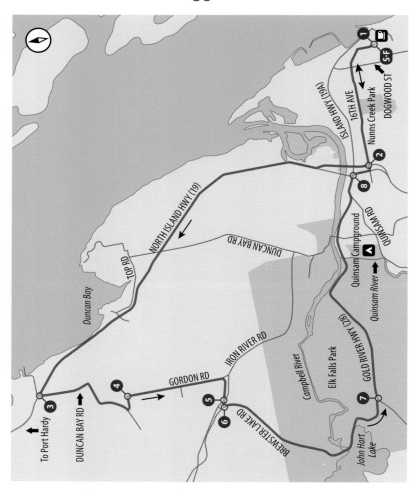

Campbell River – North Loop

DISTANCE	23km/14mi.
LEVEL	Easy to moderate.
HIGHLIGHTS	Gordon Road; John Heart Lake and dam; Elk Falls Provincial Park.
START	Campbell River visitor centre and the Tyee Plaza parking area.

The route

① From the parking area turn R onto Shoppers Row, which quickly becomes 16th Avenue. Keep to 16th Avenue as it bears left to take you to the edge of town.

② (2.2km/1.4mi) Turn R onto the traffic-light-controlled one-way Tamarac Street, which is northbound Highway 19 to Port Hardy. After 250m/yd, cross the also traffic-lighted junction with Highway 19A (aka Campbell River Road and Gold River Highway). You are now on Highway 19 in the direction of Port Hardy.

③ (9.6km/6mi) After a steady but gentle 7km/4.3mi climb out of Campbell River, turn L onto Duncan Bay Road. (This road starts out passing through an industrial complex but eventually becomes less cluttered.)

④ (11.3km/7.0mi) As Duncan Bay Road becomes a gravel road, you turn sharp L onto Gordon Road. In contrast to Duncan Bay Road this is a pleasant country road with a number of larger properties.

⑤ (13.6km/8.5mi) After a long R bend, cross Iron River Road at a stop sign and, 100m/yd farther, at the next stop sign, turn L onto Brewster Lake Road.

⑥ (15.6km/9.7mi) You now begin to ride along the shore of John Hart Lake and its dam for the next kilometre or so. (The road's namesake, Brewster Lake, is some 15km/9mi northwest of the dam.) Just before you bear R over a long bridge is the main entrance to Elk Falls Provincial Park. From the parking lot you can access a number of park's trails. The park's suspension bridge is not for vertigo sufferers!

⑦ (16.8km/10.4mi) At the next junction turn L onto Highway 28 riding down the long hill to the highway's junction with Highway 19.

⑧ (21.1km/13.1mi) Turn R onto the one-way Highway 19 and then, after 200m/yd, turn L at the next light onto 16th Avenue to ride the remaining 2km/1.4mi or so back to the ride's start in downtown Campbell River.

Campbell River's artistic side.

PART SEVEN: GOLD RIVER

Regarded as the geographical centre of Vancouver Island, Gold River is, in reality, firmly established as an important community on and major portal to the Island's fabled West Coast.

Gold River is not a large town (it only has a little over 1,200 inhabitants) and its economic boom years are long past. The almost total demise of the local logging industry and the shuttering of its pulp mill in 1998 were major blows. People left in droves but the ones who stayed realized the potential of the town's spectacular geographic beauty to form its economic base. Its proximity to Muchalat Inlet, Nootka Sound, Nootka Island and its now famous trail, the surrounding high mountains and especially those of Strathcona Provincial Park were viewed as grist for the town's economic future.

So if you're so inclined, you can use the town as a base from which to hike, climb, paddle, fish or even take a cruise on the MV *Uchuck III* to Yuquot (or Friendly Cove as it's sometimes called), the site of Chief Maquinna's welcoming of Captain James Cook in 1778.

Maquinna's people – the Mowachaht/Muchalaht of the Nuu-chah-nulth nation – continue to nurture their culture throughout the area and especially in Yuquot. The Yuquot Historic Village is visible homage to the people's history and culture. Their enterprise has created a sustainable economy based on the attraction of their home to the world at large. See their website at yuquot.ca.

Downtown Gold River!

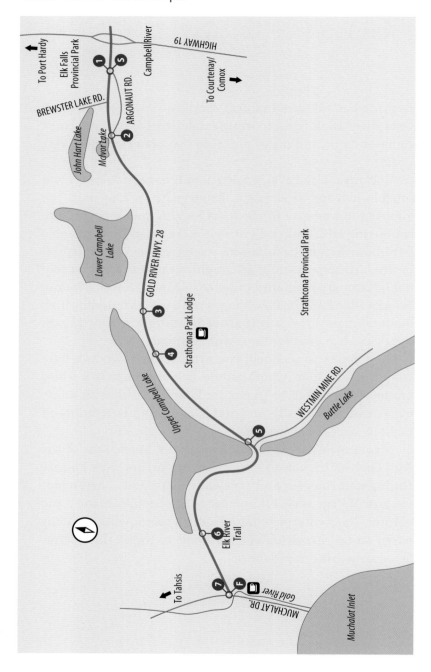

Campbell River to Gold River

Distance	87km/54mi.
Level	Strenuous
Highlights	Strathcona Provincial Park; Strathcona Park Lodge; long lakes; mountain views; gateway to Muchalat Inlet and Yuquot (Friendly Cove).
Start	Campbell River visitor centre, downtown Campbell River.

The route (follow route 38 to checkpoint 2 to get out of town)

① (3km/2mi)   You are now on Highway 28. The road to your L is Quinsam Road. If you want to avoid the long climb (3km/2mi), take this much flatter road that joins the highway 8km/5mi farther along.

② (11km/6.8mi)   Quinsam Road, now Argonaut Road, joins the highway on your L.

③ (33km/20.5mi)   Shores of Upper Campbell Lake come into view on your R.

④ (41km/25.5mi)   Pass Strathcona Park Lodge on your R.

⑤ (47km/29mi)   Turn R to cross the Buttle Narrows bridge. The road that continues straight leads to the Westmin Mine and into the heart of Strathcona Provincial Park.

⑥ (70.6km/43.8mi) Pass the Elk River Trailhead on your L.

⑦ (87km/54mi)   After a short descent follow the highway as it enters the town of Gold River.

For those riders who want to go farther, Muchalat Inlet is 13km/8mi away at the end of the highway. The MV *Uchuck III* sails from the marina here. Also, the town's municipal campground is 4km/2.5mi along this road on your L (beside the river).

Opposite: *Canoeists entering Buttle Lake from Upper Campbell Lake.*
Top: *The Gold River Boot.*
Bottom: *Storm brewing?*

PART EIGHT: PORT ALICE

Sitting on the shores of Neroutsos Inlet – a long, slender extension of Quatsino Sound – Port Alice is a little over 50km/31mi southwest of Port Hardy at the butt-end of Highway 30. (From the junction of Highway 19 it's a 30km/18.7mi ride.)

Once a thriving pulp-mill town, Port Alice, sans pulp mill, now relies on its natural beauty, abundance of wild life (think bear, sea otter and fin fish), outdoor sports (think kayaking, scuba diving, fishing and mountain biking) and the surrounding forest (think logging) for its economic viability.

The ride along this well-maintained paved road has its fair share of hills, but they are mitigated by long avenues.of conifers (lots of cedars) and views over lakes and the Marble River.

Port Alice itself is largely set back from the inlet, with its main road paralleling the foreshore. If you ignore the patches of clear-cut on the mountains opposite, the views across the waters of the inlet are stunning and well worth the longish out-and-back ride.

vancouverislandnorth.ca

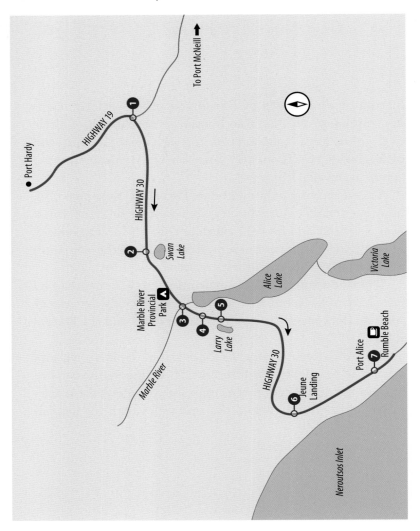

Port Hardy to Port Alice

DISTANCE	52km/32mi.
LEVEL	Moderate to strenuous.
HIGHLIGHTS	Marble River, Alice Lake.
START	From Carrot Park in front of the "Welcome to Port Hardy" sign on Market Street, head south on Market Street. After a long L curve, Market becomes Rupert Street, which soon morphs into Hardy Bay Road. Follow Hardy Bay Road to its junction with Douglas Street, aka Highway 19. Turn L onto the highway and ride the almost 18km/11mi to the junction of Highway 30. Turn R and follow the checkpoints to Port Alice, 31km/19mi away. (The checkpoints start at kilometre 21.5/mile 13.4.)

The route

① (21.5/13.4mi)   Turn R onto Highway 30, the road to Port Alice.

② (34.5km/21.5mi)   After about 13km/8mi along this undulating, tree-lined road, you get a brief glimpse of Sara Lake on your L.

③ (36.2km/22.5mi)   Cross the Marble River. Just after the bridge, the Marble River camping area is on your R. To the L is a river access ramp.

④ (38.6km/24.0mi)   On your L is an informal viewing area over the north end of Alice Lake.

⑤ (41.0km/25.5mi)   On a long R curve you pass the south end of Larry Lake.

⑥ (50.4km/31.3mi)   After a longish downhill the road bears L to run along the shore of Neroutsos Inlet, an almost 30km/18.5mi extension of Quatsino Sound.

⑦ (52.0km/13.3mi) The village of Port Alice is on your L. A store, café, bank and liquor outlet are up a slight rise after the village's fire hall and office.

Opposite: *On the road to Port Alice.*
Top: *Neroutsos Inlet, Port Alice.*
Bottom: *Neroutsos Inlet.*

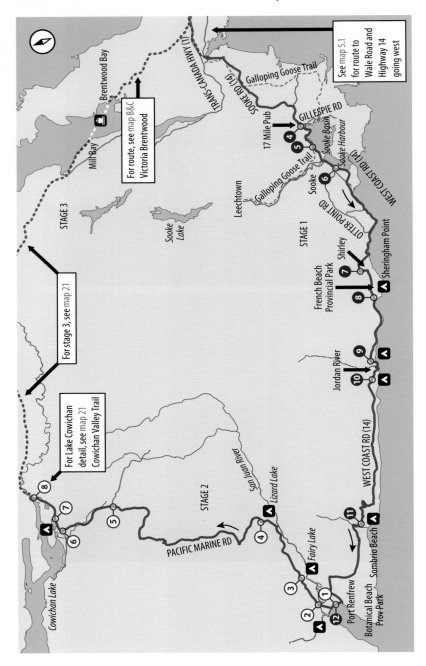

See map 5.1 for route to Wale Road and Highway 14 going west

Brentwood Bay

Galloping Goose Trail

TRANS-CANADA HWY (1)

SOOKE RD (14)

GILLESPIE RD

17 Mile Pub

Sooke Basin

Sooke Harbour

Mill Bay

For route, see map B&C Victoria Brentwood

Sooke

STAGE 3

Leechtown

Galloping Goose Trail

Sooke Lake

STAGE 1

OTTER POINT RD

WEST COAST RD (14)

Sheringham Point

Shirley

French Beach Provincial Park

For stage 3, see map 21

Jordan River

For Lake Cowichan detail, see map 21 Cowichan Valley Trail

San Juan River

Lizard Lake

STAGE 2

Fairy Lake

WEST COAST RD (14)

PACIFIC MARINE RD

Cowichan Lake

Port Renfrew

Sombrio Beach

Botanical Beach Prov Park

PART NINE: SELECTED LONGER ROUTES

Victoria / Port Renfrew / Victoria Loop

I've described this tour as a three-day affair but I know people who have done it in one day on their road bikes. Needless to say, they have other reasons to do the ride than just the scenery. Even over three days it's not the most leisurely of rides, but given the paucity of settlements, it's difficult to plan it otherwise unless you're camping.

The three stages of the tour are a study in contrasts and each has its own appeal. First is the mostly coastal route that is never too far from the shores of the Strait of Juan de Fuca. Next is the ride through the Seymour Range, a collection of mountains and hills between the coast and Lake Cowichan. Third is the uniformly flat trail that runs along the northern edge of the Cowichan Valley. Last is the short stretch of highway before the ferry journey and then the pleasant ride back to Victoria.

renfrewchamber.com

sooke-portrenfrew.com

TOTAL DISTANCE	250km/155mi.
LEVEL	Moderate to strenuous.
HIGHLIGHTS	Oceanside road; forested roads; access to provincial parks; mountain vistas; groomed linear trail; lakeside eating; "miles from anywhere" feeling; ferry ride.

STAGE 1: VICTORIA TO PORT RENFREW

The road from Victoria to Port Renfrew is, for a cyclist, one of the most challenging on southern Vancouver Island.

If the weather co-operates, the road's incessant ups and downs are compensated by glorious views to the south over the Juan de Fuca Strait and the Olympic Mountains. And it's not surprising that the road, following as it does so close to the ocean, dips down and crosses every creek and river that flows from the upland mountains and drains into the strait.

Once you leave Sooke there are no large settlements until Port Renfrew. Shirley is centred around Shirley Delicious, a popular tourist café, and the Sheringham Point lighthouse is close by. Jordan River has the air of an abandoned village with demolished houses and buildings lining its rather striking shoreline.

Apart from a few resorts along the route, the flourishing places are the provincial parks. French Beach Provincial Park is a favourite of day trippers and campers. China Beach, part of Juan de Fuca Provincial Park, is the southeast terminus of the Juan de Fuca Marine Trail, a 48km/30mi-long jaunt along the northern shores of the Strait (Botanical Beach is its northwest terminus).

Port Renfrew, once known only for its fishing and logging industries, is now a hub of ecotourism. Hikers start or finish the world-renowned West Coast Trail from here. The surrounding rainforest has become more economically sustainable as a tourist attraction than as a source of timber.

The Pacheedaht First Nation has a thriving community adjacent to Port Renfrew, with fishing and tourism as main elements of their economy.

The route

①   Leave Victoria on the Galloping Goose Regional Trail from the Johnson Street Bridge.

② (4.0km/2.5mi)   Turn L on the continuation of the "Goose" after the Switch Bridge over the Trans-Canada Highway. Follow this paved trail for 15 kilometres/9.3 miles.

③ (15km/9.3mi)   Turn L onto Wale Road, ride the 100 metres/yards to the traffic lights and turn R onto Sooke Road (aka Highway 14).

④ (31km/19.2mi)   Pass the 17 Mile House Pub on your R.

⑤ (38km/23.6mi)   Cross the Sooke River bridge. The road to your R just before the bridge, at Sooke River Road, is the access to Sooke Potholes Provincial Park.

⑥ (40km/25mi)   Continue past the roundabout in Sooke, a community of about 13,000 people. Sooke Road/Highway 14 is now also known as West Coast Road.

⑦ (59km/36.5mi)   At the top of a steep hill is the small village of Shirley. On the L is Sheringham Point Road, which leads to the Sheringham Point lighthouse. There's a café on the R corner of the highway and Sheringham Point Road called "Shirley Delicious." It's one of only two food outlets (not counting resorts) between Sooke and Port Renfrew.

⑧ (62km/38.5mi)   Entrance to French Beach Provincial Park on your L.

⑨ (73km/45.4mi)   Ride through the tiny community of Jordan River. As the road crosses the river and turns north (R) there's the tongue-in-cheek-named "Cold Shoulder Café," the second and last food outlet before Port Renfrew 30-odd kilometres away.

⑩ (76km/47mi)   On the L is the entrance to the Juan de Fuca Provincial Park campground. A kilometre farther is the road L to the park's China Beach day use area and trailhead for the Juan de Fuca Marine Trail.

⑪ (92km/51mi)   The access to Sombrio Beach L. Sombrio Beach is a favourite with the surfing community. It's also a camping stop for through hikers on the Juan de Fuca Marine Trail.

⑫ (110km/68.4mi)   Enter Port Renfrew. Unless you're staying in Port Renfrew proper or visiting the town or are heading to Botanical Beach (trailhead for the Juan de Fuca Marine Trail), turn R onto Deering Road and, after crossing the bridge over part of the San Juan River estuary, pass through the First Nation village of Pacheedaht. (There's a large campground here.)

STAGE 2: PORT RENFREW TO LAKE COWICHAN

Don't be fooled by the roughly seven kilometres/four miles of mercifully flat road after leaving Port Renfrew – it doesn't last. The sign that reads "CAUTION NARROW WINDING ROAD NEXT 26 KM" tells it all.

Top: *The view at Jordan River.*

Although the road's many hills (up and down) will maintain your average speed well below the first section of this tour, it's a road worth riding.

You'll pass two small lakes early on – Fairy and Lizard – both worth a stop. (Both have primitive campgrounds.)

This being logging country, the landscape is marked by clear-cuts large and small. Fortunately, if you try hard enough, they don't completely detract from its innate beauty.

There are no amenities along Pacific Marine Road between Port Renfrew and Mesachie Lake (and no store until Lake Cowichan), so make sure you're provisioned on leaving Renfrew.

DISTANCE	60km/37mi

The route

①		Leave Port Renfrew on Deering Road and ride to its junction with Pacific Marine Road.
②	(3.0km/1.8mi)	Turn R at the well-signed junction onto Pacific Marine Road.
③	(6.5km/4mi)	Pass the entrance to Fairy Lake on your R. (Notice "The Tree.")
④	(17.5km/10.9mi)	Pass the entrance to Lizard Lake, again on R.
⑤	(27km/16.8mi)	Sign for Tree Hill R. Given the terrain, the sign is rather redundant. After an initial kilometre or so of flattish road, the hill starts and lasts for a good four kilometres/two and a half miles.
⑥	(53.5km/33.2mi)	Turn R at the junction of Pacific Marine Road and South Shore Road.

Top: *Tree survivor.*
Bottom: *Bridge over the San Juan River estuary.*

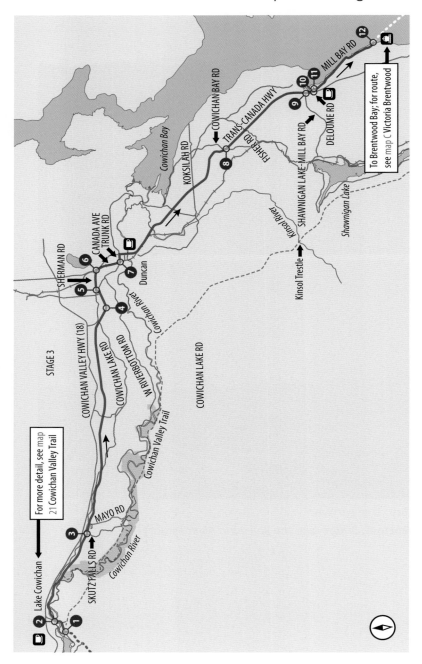

⑦ (58.3km/36.2mi)   Pass Lakeview Park Road on your L.
                      (To park and campground.)
⑧ (60km/37mi)   Enter Lake Cowichan.

STAGE 3: LAKE COWICHAN TO VICTORIA VIA DUNCAN AND MILL BAY/BRENTWOOD BAY FERRY

After two days of hilly terrain (more or less, depending on your inclination), the ride from Lake Cowichan to Duncan is ridiculously flat. Although there are two alternative routes to Duncan: the Cowichan Valley Highway (18) and Cowichan Lake Road. The one described here is the old railway grade that is now the well-groomed Cowichan Valley Trail (also part of the Trans Canada Trail). Riding the trail is a treat. You travel along avenues of trees, pass homesteads and open fields and cross a short trestle just before hitting the road that takes you into downtown Duncan.

On your journey from Duncan to Mill Bay the contrast to the delightful trail couldn't be more stark. Your path is along the shoulder of the Trans-Canada Highway, which is broad and safe enough despite the traffic. After Mill Bay you're on a much quieter shoreline road for the 5km/3mi stretch to the Mill Bay ferry terminal.

From the Brentwood Bay ferry terminal to downtown Victoria the route follows roads and then the paved Galloping Goose Regional Trail (on which you left town at the beginning of your tour). Both are well used by local cyclists. The "share the road" mentality is well-established here, so your ride into Victoria should be a pleasant one.

| DISTANCE | 80km/50mi |

The route

①   Leave Lake Cowichan from the town's visitor centre in Saywell Park on

South Shore Road, which eventually becomes Cowichan Lake Road, and ride east to the edge of town.

② (1.3km/800yd) Turn R onto Greendale Road and then immediately L onto the well-signed Cowichan Valley Trail. You'll stay on this well-maintained trail for almost 27km/16mi.

③ (9.0km/5.5mi) Cross Skutz Falls Road (the falls are 3km/1.9mi away to your R). Over the next 16.5km/10.2mi you cross five roadways: Mayo, Paldi and Cowichan Lake (the latter three times).

④ (26.5km/16.5mi) Descend a steep gully, cross a wooden bridge and then climb the equally steep exit from the gully. (It's no more than 60m/yd from side to side.)

⑤ (28.0km/17.4mi) This is the eastern terminus of the trail. Turn R onto Sherman Road. You are now on the outskirts of Duncan.

⑥ (29.0km/18.0mi) After a longish descent turn R at a roundabout onto Canada Avenue and ride the one kilometre/0.6 mile into downtown Duncan.

⑦ (30.0km/18.6mi) Just past the town's refurbished station/museum, turn L onto Trunk Road and ride 400m/yd to turn R onto the Trans-Canada Highway (1).

⑧ (37.0km/23mi) Cross the traffic-lighted Bench Road. (For the next 13.0km/8.0mi you'll cross five major intersections: Koksilah Road, Cobble Hill/Cowichan Bay roads junction, Fisher Road, Hutchinson Road and Cobble Hill/Kilmalu roads junction).

⑨ (50.0km/31.0mi)   Pass through this penultimate traffic-lighted intersection (Shawnigan Lake–Mill Bay Road goes R) and be ready to move into the L turning lane before the next traffic light.

⑩ (50.5km/31.7mi)   Turn L at this lighted junction onto Deloume Road (caution – this is a busy junction) and ride the 100m/yd down to Mill Bay Road.

⑪ (51.0km/31.7mi)   Turn R onto Mill Bay Road. (There's a large shopping centre on your R. Cheaper ferry tickets can be bought at Thrifty Foods.)

⑫ (57.0km/35.4mi)   Turn L at the stop sign and ride down to the Mill Bay ferry terminal. (The ferry to Brentwood Bay takes about 25 minutes and runs roughly every 1½ hours from 8 a.m. to 6:30 p.m. Check bcferries.com for exact times.

BRENTWOOD BAY FERRY TERMINAL TO DOWNTOWN VICTORIA

For the route from the Brentwood Bay ferry terminal into Victoria, a distance of 22km/14mi, see map C.

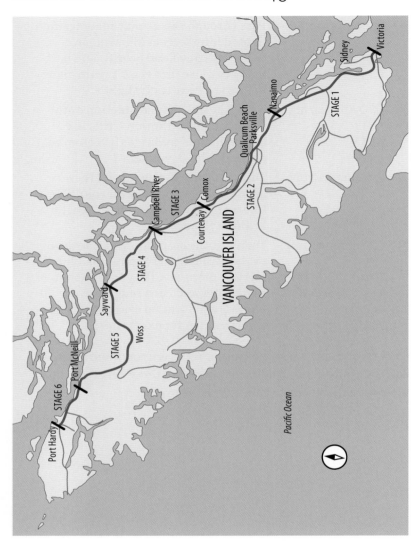

Victoria to Port Hardy

This, the longest route by far in the book, is one of those journeys that can define your bike-touring escapades for years. It has many of the characteristics we cyclists look for in a longish tour. It's physically challenging and has spectacular scenery with enough pleasant towns and villages to make stops and overnighters worthwhile. Apart from one exception, each of the six stages ends in a sizable community that offers the curious cyclist enough interest to be satisfied. Also, there's always a selection of grocery stores, restaurants and cafés so you won't starve. And it's that one exception, stage 5, that might take you out of your comfort zone trying to complete it in a day. There is an escape strategy, though: staying overnight at Woss. But you will want to make sure you have your night's accommodation secured before you set off.

As you ride north and as you leave the main thoroughfare, Highway 19, you'll be aware of the string of linear settlements that line the road. Many are attractive seaside communities; others are unremarkable places with no discernible reason for their existence, at least from an outsider's perspective.

Note that accommodation is sparse north of Campbell River, as are convenience stores and cafés. Make sure you have enough supplies for at least a few days. If you're camping you might have to detour off the main road to a recreation site.

Although I've described each stage from the perspective of riding Highway 19, aka Island Highway or Inland Island Highway, and Highway 19A, aka Oceanside Route, I have marked on the maps alternative routes you might take, particularly in the southern half of the Island. These routes, if taken, will of course add more kilometres/miles to your day's distances. If you are tempted to veer off the main route, you can find detailed route descriptions by consulting the routes

I've described for each of the main communities you'll pass on your way north.

portmcneill.net

porthardychamber.com

TOTAL DISTANCE	524km/325mi

STAGE 1: VICTORIA TO NANAIMO

Unless you've decided to take the Brentwood Bay/Mill Bay ferry to get you to Mill Bay, you will encounter "the Malahat," a stretch of mostly uphill road that takes you out of town. Not only is it hilly, it's the only road from Victoria to the rest of the Island's east-side communities. That means it's busy. So be prepared. After Mill Bay, the road settles down and you're riding on the wide shoulder of what is commonly called the "Island Highway."

The first major town you ride through is Duncan, the commercial centre of the Cowichan Valley. It's known as an Indigenous cultural and entrepreneurial hub, as the local tribes constitute the largest First Nation in the province. Exquisitely carved totem poles are displayed around the town and are one of its defining features.

Ladysmith has its town centre just off the highway. Once a coal port, it's now a rather sleepy little town despite its revitalized main street. The notorious coal baron James Dunsmuir built the place and named it after the South African town where the British defeated the Boers during the Boer War.

The stage ends in Nanaimo, the second-largest community on the Island. Although its economy is very diversified today, it wasn't always that way. When James Douglas heard that coal had been discovered in the area (actually, a local Indigenous man had shown one of his roving assistants a piece of coal), he instigated the beginning of the Island's coal mining industry. That was in 1852. Nanaimo's coal mining

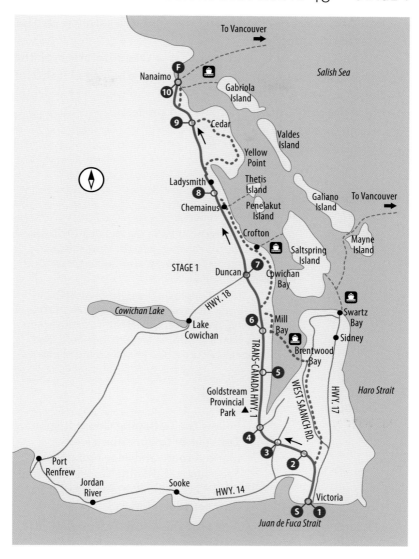

lasted for almost a century and was the city's raison d'être for most of that time.

The city's name, "Nanaimo," is a transliteration of the name of the Snunéymuxw tribe, the original inhabitants of the area. They are Coast Salish people who were very welcoming of the early British colonials and settlers.

tourismvictoria.com

tourismcowichan.com

tourismnanaimo.com

DISTANCE	114km/70mi.
LEVEL	Moderate to strenuous.
HIGHLIGHTS	Goldstream Provincial Park; the Malahat Drive; the Malahat summit; roadside market stores; nearby wineries; interesting downtown of Duncan; historic downtown Nanaimo.
START	Johnson Street Bridge, on the edge of downtown Victoria. (If you want to avoid the 24-kilometre/15-mile climb up and over the Malahat, take the Brentwood Bay–Mill Bay ferry to Mill Bay (see Ferry and Airport Access Route C and join the route at checkpoint 6.)

The route

①		Follow the Galloping Goose Regional Trail out of town. (This a well-marked route and easy to navigate. See route 5 Galloping Goose Regional Trail / Lochside Regional Trail for a complete description.)
②	(10.0km/6.2mi)	Just past the 10km trail marker (R) (at 100m/yd or so) and next to the Trans-Canada Highway overpass, find a short paved trail going to Watkiss Way. Turn L here and ride a further 200m/yd to a bus shelter and turn L

Top: *Farmers Market along the Island Highway.*
Bottom: *View from the Malahat over the Saanich Inlet.*

again onto a narrow paved path up to the Trans-Canada Highway and turn R to ride on the highway's wide shoulder.

③ (13.6km/8.4mi) Pass the Millstream Road intersection (Exit 14) with care.

④ (20.2km/12.5mi) Pass the entrance to Goldstream Provincial Park.

⑤ (32.5km/20.2mi) The Malahat summit (352m/1155ft).

⑥ (42.9km/26.6mi) Pass by the small community of Mill Bay.

⑦ (63.3km/39.3mi) Trunk Road, Duncan. Turn L here for the town's centre.

⑧ (92.0km/57.2mi) Ladysmith. The town centre is off to the L. Below the highway, on the R, is Transfer Beach Park. Ten kilometres/ six miles on, pass Nanaimo Airport on your R.

⑨ (100.3km/63.2mi) Rather than pass under the Nanaimo Parkway to continue on the Trans-Canada, stay R and take the off ramp signed for Parksville and Campbell River. About 70m/yd along the ramp take the signed path down to the R onto Cedar Road. Cross Cedar Road (with care), riding to your L, and then turn R to rejoin the Trans-Canada.

⑩ (114.0km/70.8mi) Nanaimo town centre. The old town is on the R. The ferry to Vancouver leaves from Departure Bay 3km/1.8mi north of downtown.

STAGE 2: NANAIMO TO COURTENAY

Your journey to Courtenay starts by negotiating Nanaimo's traffic (even if you choose the bike path out of town).

However, it's not too long before you're riding along the shores of Nanoose Bay and then past the entrance to Rathtrevor Beach Provincial Park on your R. (This is worth a visit. Its campground set among towering Douglas firs and its 2km(1.2mi) sandy beach are a treat after the noisy highway.) Parksville's claim to fame is as a tourist and retirement centre. Its proximity to two largish parks – Rathtrevor Beach mentioned above and the Englishman River Regional Park – and the town's own sandy beaches are major draws. After Parksville there follows a series of small coastal communities, some defined by their scalloped beaches, others being residential enclaves.

Between Bowser and Union Bay you get tantalizing views of the two most northerly of the Gulf Islands: Denman and Hornby. Both have interesting communities, and their roads are a joy to ride, despite being rather lumpy.

The triplet communities of Courtenay, Comox and Cumberland are collectively known as the Comox Valley. Courtenay is the largest of the three. Cumberland is the smallest. Comox has a busy marina and has a large Canadian Forces base on the edge of town. Topographically the whole region is dominated by the Comox Glacier, a massive dome of rock and ice. The local First Nation call the glacier Kwénis, meaning whale. In their legend of the "Great Flood" a whale became trapped on the mountain as the waters receded. Both Courtenay and Comox are situated on the shores of the large estuary of the Puntledge and Tsolum rivers known as Comox Harbour.

parksvillechamber.com
discovercomoxvalley.com

DISTANCE	108km/67mi.
LEVEL	Moderate.
HIGHLIGHTS	Rathtrevor Beach Provincial Park; beaches of

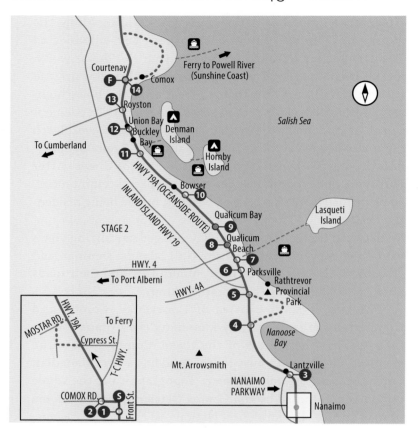

Nanoose Bay, Parksville, Qualicum Beach, Qualicum Bay, Union Bay and Royston; Denman and Hornby islands and their parks; Courtenay's compact town centre and its riverside Lewis Park; Comox marina.

START   The Bastion on Front Street in downtown Nanaimo.

The route

①   Ride north on Front Street and then bear L onto Comox Road.

② (600m/yd)   Turn R onto the Trans-Canada Highway. After 200m/yd, keep L as the Trans-Canada Highway veers R down to the Departure Bay ferry terminal. You're now on Highway 19, aka Island Highway. This is a busy road with numerous intersections until you leave town. (There's a bike path you can access by turning L on Cypress Street about 1.5km/1mi from your turn onto the highway and then R onto the bike path a short distance on this dead-end street. This will take you roughly 10km/6mi to Mostar Road, where you turn R to rejoin the highway.)

③ (13.4km/8.3mi)   Merge with traffic coming off Nanaimo Parkway.

④ (24.3km/15.1mi) Pass the intersection with Northwest Bay Road, the road into Nanoose Bay. Climbing from the intersection, you're able to see the 1819m/5,967ft Mt. Arrowsmith off to your L.

⑤ (30.4km/18.9mi) Take the off ramp (exit 46) to follow the Old Island Highway, also named Highway 19A and signed as the Oceanside Route, into Parksville.

⑥ (36.0km/22.4mi)   Parksville. At the road's junction with Alberni Way, aka Highway 4A to Port Alberni, you're as close as you get to the core of this small town. A few metres/yards on your R is a beach access off Beachside Drive.

⑦ (40.5km/25mi)   Pass Lee Road, the access to the Lasqueti Island passenger ferry terminal on your R.

⑧ (46.7km/29mi)   Qualicum Beach. You're at the junction of Highway 4, another road to Port Alberni. Turning L here will take you into the small town's centre, 2km/1.3mi away.

⑨ (60.6km/37.6mi)   Pass the intersection with Horne Lake Road (L). (The Horne Lake caves are a favourite with spelunkers.) Qualicum Bay is a short distance past this intersection.

⑩ (67.4km/41.9mi)   Bowser. There are two small grocery stores either side of the highway in this small community.

⑪ (86.2km/53.5mi)   Buckley Bay. This is the ferry terminal for Denman and Hornby islands. These two islands are well worth a visit. Both have provincial parks: Fillongley and Boyle Point on Denman; Tribune Bay and Helliwell on Hornby.

⑫ (93.0km/57.8mi)   Union Bay. An old coal-shipping town. You'll ride by its turn-of-the-twentieth-century schoolhouse, post office and church, which are still in use. Views to the east over Denman Island and the Coast Mountains beyond.

Top: *Chrome Island off the southern tip of Denman.*
Bottom: *Mt. Arrowsmith from the Island Highway.*

⑬ (102.0km/63.3mi)   Royston. A main road to Cumberland
                       (7.0km/4.3mi away) goes to the L at
                       the traffic-lighted junction in the
                       centre of this seaside village.

⑭ (108.3km/67.3mi)   Courtenay town centre. To visit
                       the town of Comox and its marina,
                       5.0km/3.0mi away, turn R onto 17th
                       Street just before the town centre and
                       follow the Comox signs.

STAGE 3: COURTENAY TO CAMPBELL RIVER

This short ride affords plenty of opportunities to stop and explore. Even if you don't do that, it'll give you lots of time to poke about Campbell River. The two most attractive places on the route are Miracle Beach Provincial Park and the beaches of Oyster Bay and Willow Point. The park has a long pebble and sand beach and the estuary for Black Creek is on its northern boundary. Just after crossing the Oyster River the highway cleaves closely to the shoreline for almost 20km/12mi until Campbell River's town centre. The exposed beaches of Oyster Bay and Willow Point give grand views over the northern reaches of the Salish Sea and its islands and to the Sunshine Coast and the Coast Mountains beyond.

Campbell River is a town of just over 35,000 people and is a gateway to the northeast and northwest of the Island (including the northern portion of Strathcona Provincial Park) and the Discovery Islands, especially Quadra and Cortes. Although its glory days as a logging and pulp-mill town are over, it still maintains its boast as the "Salmon Capital of the World." That boast and the town's proximity to some of the Island's most beautiful mountains and coastlines draw visitors from all over the world. Its compact downtown is easy to navigate and its three harbours give the place an authentic waterfront-town ambiance.

campbellriver.travel

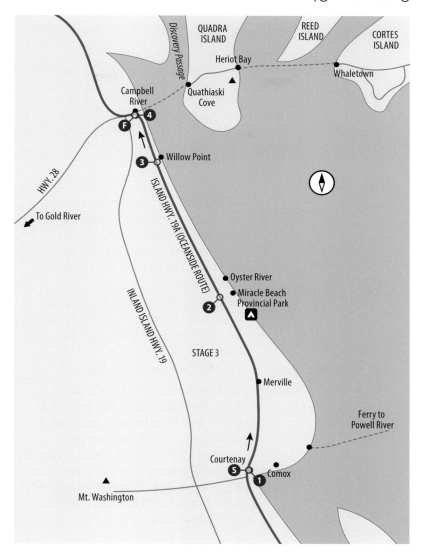

DISTANCE	46km/28.5mi.
LEVEL	Easy to moderate.
HIGHLIGHTS	Miracle Beach Provincial Park; Oyster Bay and Willows Point beaches; views over to the Sunshine Coast, Desolation Sound, Quadra, Cortes and Savary islands; Campbell River's Robert V. Ostler Park.
START	Downtown Courtenay, corner of 5th Street and Cliffe Avenue.

The route

① Ride north on 5th Street and cross the Puntledge River Bridge on the road out of town. At the third set of traffic lights continue straight as the Highway 19A bypass joins the road from the R.

② (23km/14.3mi) Pass Miracle Beach Drive on your R. This is the access road to Miracle Beach Provincial Park, 2.0km/1.3mi away.

③ (38.5km/24mi) Pass Willow Point beaches.

④ (46km/28.5mi) Campbell River's visitor centre, 300m/yd past where Highway 19A turns R to bypass the town centre. Campbell River is the start of Highway 28 to Gold River and Nootka Sound (Yuquot/Friendly Cove). The highway is also the gateway into Elk Falls Provincial Park and Strathcona Provincial Park.

STAGE 4: CAMPBELL RIVER TO SAYWARD

The highway north from Campbell River can be a lonely road. But most of us cyclists are used to "lonely." In fact, we embrace it. There's something about being alone on our touring bike – alone in our mind, alone in our body's exertion, with the asphalt leading us on to who knows where – that is deeply nourishing. That's what can happen once you leave Campbell River and begin pedalling your way toward Sayward. Though the highway is not straight or flat, the phalanxes of fir, hemlock and spruce trees on either side give the impression of riding through a landscape of nothing else but trees and, if it were not for the traffic, of unbelievable isolation. That's not to imply there are no mountain vistas. There are. But not as frequent as one would want.

Then, out of all this isolation, comes Roberts Lake and its reassurance that there are humans about. Its homey resort comes almost at the halfway point of the journey to Sayward.

Sayward has a small population of about 300. It has a spectacular setting, being surrounded by mountains, the coastal waters of Johnstone Strait and the wide estuary of the Salmon River. The town is dominated to its south by Mt. H'Kusam, a 1645m/5397ft peak. The climb up and over has been popularized by the endurance event called the Kusam Klimb.

sayward.ca

DISTANCE	75km/45mi.
LEVEL	Moderate.
HIGHLIGHTS	Roberts Lake; Sayward Village and Kelsey Bay's waterfront; semi-remote highway.
START	Campbell River's visitor centre.

The route

 From the roadway side of the visitor centre, ride north on Shoppers Row (aka 16th Street) for 500m/yd and turn R onto Dogwood Street. After 300m/yd turn L onto Highway 19A.

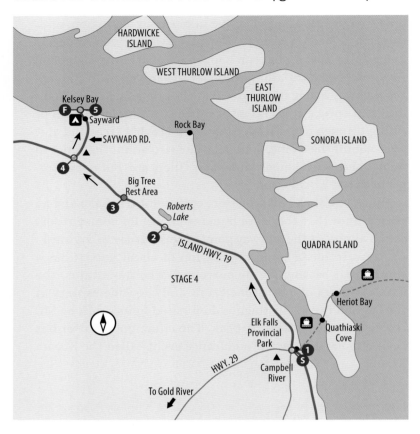

Unexpected delight along the Island Highway.

		After a further 2km/1.2mi turn R onto Highway 19 and leave town. (Going straight is Highway 28 to Gold River.)
②	(30km/18.6mi)	Pass Roberts Lake and rest area.
③	(45.6km/28.3mi)	Big Tree rest area.
④	(63.0km/39.1mi)	At Sayward Junction turn R onto Sayward Road. There are good facilities here: groceries, restaurant, camping and motel. There are also some services a short distance away in Sayward.
⑤	(73.0km/45.4mi)	Turn L onto Kelsey Way, signed VILLAGE CENTRE, where you'll find shops and services. There's also a pleasant picnic area by a small lake (where camping is allowed). To visit Kelsey Bay, continue on Kelsey Way back to Sayward Road. Turn L and ride the 1.5km/1mi to the end of the road, which is ... Kelsey Bay.

STAGE 5: SAYWARD TO PORT MCNEILL

And the sense of isolation continues. Say what you like about the logging practice of clear-cutting, it does occasionally result in the possibility of seeing beyond just the road. As you ride north the mountains are sometimes revealed in all their splendour. About 20km/12mi after Sayward is the access to the Mt. Cain ski resort.

Woss is not the most attractive of settlements (it's sometimes known as Woss Lake because of its proximity to the large lake to its west). But it does have a grocery store and a motel (at least as of this writing) that can provide a touring cyclist with some respite.

Although it's a bit of a detour, the road down to Telegraph

Cove is worth the effort. The Cove in summer buzzes with nautical activities. Its proximity to Robson Bight and the Broughton Archipelago makes it an obvious staging area for kayaks, small motor craft and larger ecotourism boats to explore the surrounding waters.

Port McNeill is a short way downhill from the highway. The ride ends at the water's edge by the visitor centre, an appropriate place to ask your questions (if it's still open by the time you arrive). Like most communities on the north end of the Island, the predominant economic activity here is/was logging. Port McNeill is also the Island's ferry access to Sointula on Malcolm Island and Alert Bay on Cormorant Island – the former an old Finnish settlement with a funky, century-old co-op store; the latter, a major Kwakwaka'wakw community renowned for its U'mista Cultural Centre.

portmcneill.ca

DISTANCE	138km/86mi.
LEVEL	Moderate to strenuous.
HIGHLIGHTS	Semi-remote highway; mountains; river crossings; lakes large and small; the village of Woss (at 72km/44.7mi from Sayward, Woss makes a good destination if you don't want too long a day in the saddle); Port McNeill's waterfront and the views over Broughton Strait to Malcolm Island (Sointula) and the Coast Mountains beyond.
START	Sayward's shopping area on Kelsey Way.

The route

① Leave Sayward and retrace your route to Sayward Junction and Highway 19. Turn R. (There are a few rest areas between Sayward and Port McNeill. The first is Keta Lake at about 20km/12.4mi from Sayward.)

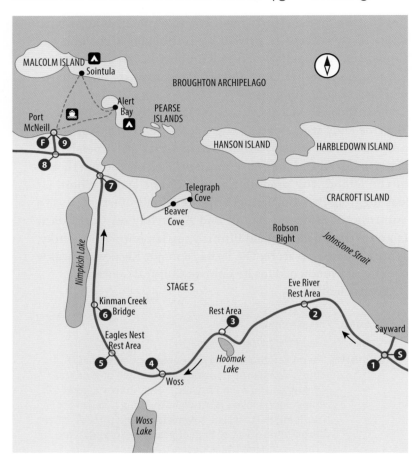

② (35km/21.7mi)   East River rest area.

③ (65.4km/40.6mi)   Hoomak Lake rest area.

④ (71.5km/44.4mi)   The village of Woss on the L. There is a general store and motel a short distance from the highway.

⑤ (77.7km/48.3mi)   Eagles Nest rest area. The highway now follows the Nimpkish River to its outlet from Nimpkish Lake. Unfortunately it's a shy river and you barely see it.

⑥ (102.6km/63.7mi)   As you cross the Kinman Creek bridge you are now at the southern end of Nimpkish Lake, which is more than 20 kilometres (12-plus miles) long. Like its namesake river, you rarely get to see this grand lake, the deepest on the Island. It's reputed to be over 1000ft (305m) at its deepest.

⑦ (128.0km/79.5mi)   Pass Beaver Cove Road on your R. Beaver Cove and Telegraph Cove are 13km and 15km (8mi and 9.3mi) away respectively, at the end of this road. The latter is well known for its ecotourism.

⑧ (135.3km/84mi)   Turn R onto Campbell Way, the main road into Port McNeill.

⑨ (138.0km/85.7mi)   Port McNeill's visitor centre, on Beach Drive close to the ferry terminal. (Ferries to Sointula, on Malcolm Island, and Alert Bay leave from here.)

STAGE 6: PORT MCNEILL TO PORT HARDY

The short but not so winding road of this last stretch of your journey will feel a little anticlimactic when compared to the

previous five stages of your ride. There's not much to divert your attention from the asphalt; not a lot of vistas to give pleasure; not much in the way of "roadside attractions." In fact, unless you pop into Fort Rupert, the road doesn't get interesting until you turn right onto Hardy Bay Road to head into the town of Port Hardy.

With over 4,000 inhabitants, Port Hardy is the largest community on northern Vancouver Island. Its nearby BC Ferries terminal at Bear Cove is the start of the 500-kilometre (310-mile), 16-hour Inside Passage route to Prince Rupert on BC's North Coast. (There is also a ferry to Bella Coola from here.) The town is regarded at the gateway to Cape Scott Provincial Park on the Island's northwestern tip, 65 kilometres (40 miles) away on a rough gravel road.

Though not endowed with many tourist attractions, the town does have a waterfront park which, when the weather is kind, is a pleasant place to picnic and gaze over the harbour to the wider waters of Queen Charlotte Strait and the Coast Mountains in the distance.

visitporthardy.com

DISTANCE	43km/27mi.
LEVEL	Easy to moderate.
HIGHLIGHTS	Fort Rupert's village and shoreline; Port Hardy's harbour and shoreline parks.
START	Port McNeill's visitor centre.

The route

①		Retrace your route along Campbell Way to Highway 19 and turn R.
②	(24.6km/15.3mi)	Pass the junction of highways 19 and 30. Highway 30 is the road to Port Alice, 30km/18.5mi away.

The long road to Port Hardy.

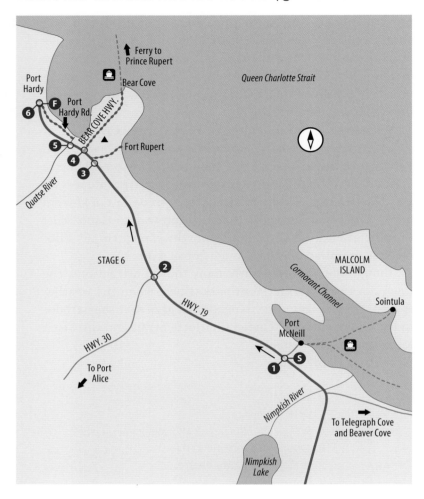

Ferry from Alert Bay arriving at Port McNeil (Sointula in the background).

③ (34.1km/21.2mi) Fort Rupert Road is on your R. Although this road is signed for the airport, it takes you to Fort Rupert.

④ (38.8km/24.1mi) Junction of Highway 19 and, yes, Highway 19, aka Douglas Street. The highway going R (aka Bear Cove Highway) goes to the BC Ferries terminal (for Prince Rupert and Bella Coola), 5km/3mi away. Continue straight on Highway 19/Douglas Street toward Port Hardy.

⑤ (40.3km/25mi) A short distance farther, and after crossing the Quatse River bridge, turn R onto Hardy Bay Road. This is a far more pleasant way into town than Douglas Street. There's also a multi-use path on the R for part of the way.

⑥ (43.5km/27mi) Port Hardy. Finish the ride by turning R onto Market Street (at the elementary school) to the town's waterfront Carrot Park.

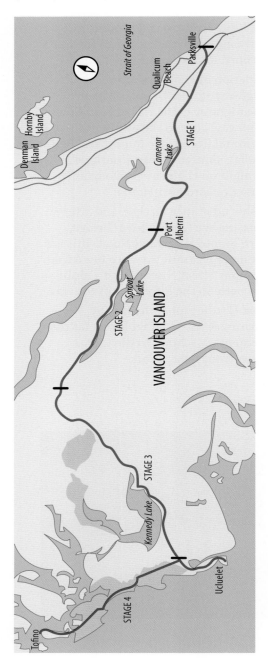

Cross-Island Tour: Parksville to Tofino / Ucluelet

Traversing Vancouver Island from the shores of the Salish Sea to the long and wild beaches of the Pacific Ocean is perhaps one of the defining cycling road tours on the west coast of the province. Though not an easy ride, it has everything a cyclist could ask for. Starting in the seaside town of Parksville, you head west to encounter high mountains, long climbs, glorious lakes, river rapids and the spectacular, windswept edge of the Island's Pacific coast.

The logistics of this route can become complicated when you consider that between the outskirts of Port Alberni and Highway 4's Tofino/Ucluelet junction – a distance of around 80km/50mi – there is no accommodation, camping or otherwise, and no food/groceries/supplies for purchase. If you're a strong rider, you should have no problem. Likewise if you have a support vehicle. But even if neither of those applies, as long as you have camping gear, good food supplies and bike repair equipment, you'll have the chance to be creative. (Although you shouldn't spread yourself out in the middle of a logging road – or even beside one, if it comes to that.)

As with other long tours in the book, I've divided this one into stages. Their delineation, as you will appreciate, is dictated not necessarily by a specific destination but by how they facilitate description of the route. For example, the Taylor River rest area is not the ideal place to end a day's ride but it does provide a logical pause in describing an otherwise long stretch of the route.

| TOTAL DISTANCE | 172km/107mi (Tofino) |
| | 147km/91mi (Ucluelet) |

DISTANCE	48km/30mi.
LEVEL	Moderate to strenuous.
HIGHLIGHTS	Old Country Market in Coombs; Little Qualicum Falls Provincial Park and campground; views of Mt. Arrowsmith; Cameron Lake; Cathedral Grove and Port Alberni.
INFORMATION	visitparksvillequalicumbeach.com albernivalleytourism.com
START	Downtown Parksville. The junction of Highway 19A (Old Island Highway) and Highway 4A (Alberni Highway).

The route

①		From the junction, ride west on the Alberni Highway out of town.
②	(2.0km/1.2mi)	Pass under the overpass of Highway 19 (Island Highway). Keep to the Alberni Highway but watch for R-turning traffic entering the Nanaimo on-ramp. Once past this junction and until you near Cameron Lake, on your L, you get views of Mt. Arrowsmith, which, at 1819m/5,968ft high, dominates the area.
③	(11.5km/7.1mi)	Having passed the village of Coombs (and its famous market with rooftop goats) 2km/1.2mi earlier, you now turn L at the traffic-light junction of Highway 4 coming in from your R.
④	(18.2km/11.3mi)	On the R is Little Qualicum Falls Road. The eponymous provincial park and campground is about 100m/yd up this road.
⑤	(22.7km/14.1mi)	The entrance to the Cameron Lake

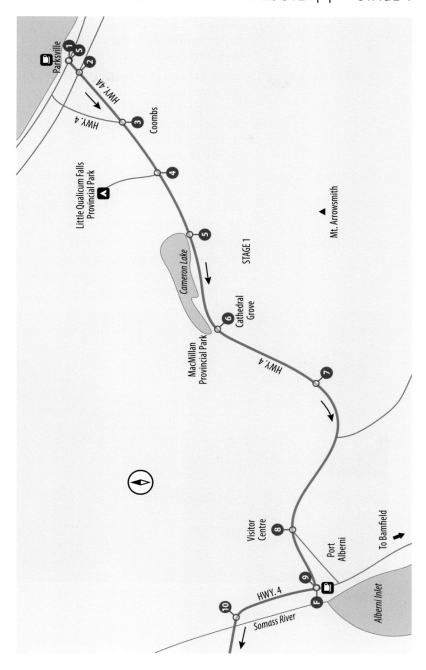

picnic ground is on your R. The road hugs the lakeshore for the next 5km/3mi or so.

(6) (28.7km/17.8mi) Enter a stand of giant Douglas fir trees known as Cathedral Grove. This is part of MacMillan Provincial Park, renowned for centuries-old and metres/yards-wide conifers. Definitely worth a stop.

(7) (34.7km/21.6mi) Since leaving Cathedral Grove, you've been climbing, inexorably, up what is locally referred to as "the hump." Now you're on your way back down.

(8) (42.6km/26.5mi) At a major junction, continue R, keeping to Highway 4, signed for Ucluelet and Tofino. The area's visitor centre is at this junction.

Above: *Cameron Lake.*
Opposite: *Cathedral Grove.*

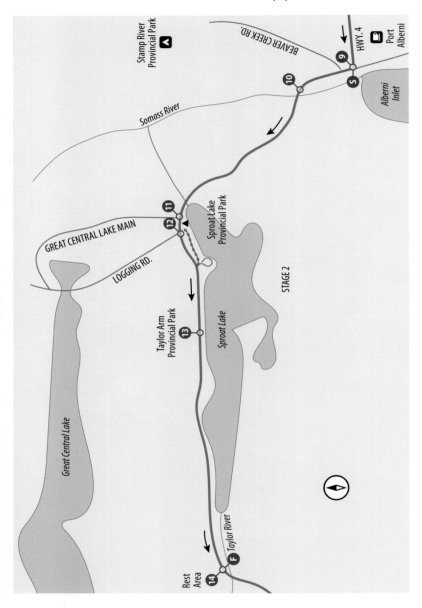

⑨ (48.1km/29.9mi)   You're now on the northwest side of Port Alberni. Turn R onto a continuation of Highway 4, also now known as the Pacific Rim Highway and locally as River Road.

STAGE 2: PORT ALBERNI TO TAYLOR RIVER REST AREA

DISTANCE	39km/24mi).
LEVEL	Easy to moderate.
HIGHLIGHTS	Sproat Lake; Sproat Lake Provincial Park; native art gallery; Taylor Arm Provincial Park.
START	Junction of Johnson Street (Highway 4) and River Road (Highway 4, aka Pacific Rim Highway). (See checkpoint 9 above.)

The route

⑩ (50.0km/31.6mi)   As you proceed along Highway 4 the road now turns L to cross the "Orange Bridge" (which isn't actually orange) over the Somass River. The Tseshaht First Nation's impressive administration building is on your L just over the bridge. And a couple of kilometres/a mile and a half farther, on your R, is the Ahtsik Native Art Gallery.

⑪ (58.3km/36.2mi)   Pass Central Lake Road (and the way to the Sproat Lake Provincial Park upper campground) on your R.

⑫ (58.7km/36.5mi)   Pass the entrance road to Sproat Lake Provincial Park's lower campground (which is smaller than the upper campground but has lake access) on your L. This access road is, in fact, Lakeshore Road and provides a marginally longer alternative route to Highway 4 a few kilometres/miles shy of the next checkpoint. Sproat Lake is now your companion for the next 20km/12mi.

(13) (69.7km/43.3mi)   On your R is the entrance to Taylor Arm Provincial Park.

(14) (88.8km/55.2mi)   The entrance to the Taylor River rest area is on your R.

STAGE 3: TAYLOR RIVER REST AREA TO PACIFIC RIM HIGHWAY / TOFINO / UCLUELET HIGHWAY JUNCTION

DISTANCE	51km/31.5mi.
LEVEL	Strenuous.
HIGHLIGHTS	Sutton Pass; snow-capped mountains; the Kennedy River rapids; Kennedy Lake and the road along the lakeshore.
START	Exit the Taylor River rest area access road onto Highway 4 and turn R. Within the next 5km/3mi you will have climbed the 175m-/574ft-high Sutton Pass on its 10 per cent grade to the summit.

The route

(15) (103.2km/64.1mi)   Having ridden over Sutton Pass, you now pass the Kennedy River Rapids at the Wally Creek bridge, a good place to rest and recover.

(16) (118.2km/73.4mi)   You get your first taste of some stiff climbs, a couple of them in the 18 per cent range. The journey from here to the junction is pretty lumpy but there is a compensation: the glorious views over Kennedy Lake, which the road accompanies, off and on, for almost 20km/12mi.

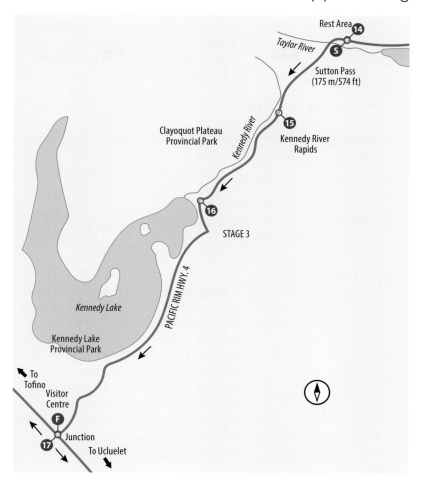

⑰ (139.7km/86.8mi) The junction of Highway 4 and the Tofino–Ucluelet Highway. The Pacific Rim visitor centre is on your R just before the junction.

STAGE 4: THE JUNCTION TO TOFINO

DISTANCE	33km/20mi.
LEVEL	Moderate.
HIGHLIGHTS	Downtown Tofino; Kʷisitis visitor centre and Wicka-ninnish beach; Long Beach; Chesterman Beach and Frank Island; Radar Hill.
START	The junction of Highway 4 and the Tofino–Ucluelet Highway.

The route

⑱ (144.5km/89.8mi) Having had to turn R at the junction on the continuation of Highway 4, you now see, on the L, Wick Road – the way to the Kʷisitis visitor centre, Florencia Bay and Wickaninnish Bay and beach a little over 3km/1.9mi away. Both bays have quintessential "wild" west coast beaches, while the visitor centre displays and depicts the inimitable place of First Nations in this amazing environment.

⑲ (152.0km/94.4mi) Entrance to Green Point campground on your L.

⑳ (155.5km/9.6mi) Entrance to Incinerator Rock and Long Beach itself on your L.

㉑ (158.5km/98.5mi) The road to Grice Bay on your R. This bay is part of the much larger Clayoquot Sound.

㉒ (162.0km/100.6mi) This road on your L is the way to Radar Hill and the Kapyong

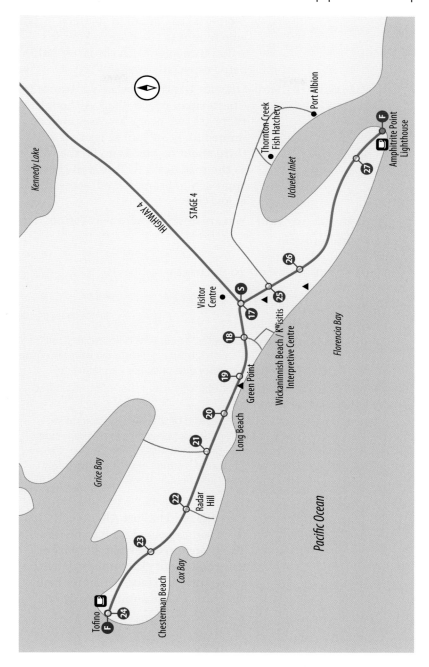

Memorial to Canadian soldiers who fought in the Korean War. It's 1.5km/1mi long, with the latter half being especially steep.

㉓ (167.0km/103.8mi) On your L is the southern entrance to Chesterman Beach Road. Although there are two beach accesses almost immediately on your L, there is a third about 0.5km/0.3mi farther on as the road bears R. This is the best approach to Frank Island, accessible at low tide.

㉔ (172.5km/107.2mi) You are now in downtown Tofino.

tourismtofino.com

STAGE 5: THE JUNCTION TO UCLUELET

DISTANCE	8km/5mi.
LEVEL	Moderate.
HIGHLIGHTS	Downtown Ucluelet; aquarium; Wild Pacific Trail; Amphitrite Point Lighthouse; Florencia Bay; Thornton Creek fish hatchery and possible bear viewing.
START	The junction of Highway 4 and the Tofino–Ucluelet Highway.
THE ROUTE	Turn L in the direction of Ucluelet. As you do so, you'll notice a multi-use paved path on the R side of the road that goes all the way to the centre of town. There are two campgrounds almost immediately to your L after the junction.

㉕ (141.0km/87.6mi) Pass the road to Port Albion (sometimes posted for Itatsoo Bay). The Thornton Creek hatchery is off this road about 5km/3mi away (with some gravel surface). Great for bear watching in late summer/early fall.

㉖ (141.7km/88.0mi)   A short distance farther, on your R, is Willowbrae Road. This gravel route leads to a trailhead for the south end of Florencia Bay and the Wya Point resort and campground.

㉗ (147.5km/91.6mi)   Main Street Ucluelet is on your L. This street goes to the water's edge and, not surprisingly, the town's aquarium.

Somewhere as you're riding into town, the Tofino–Ucluelet Highway becomes Peninsula Road. If you continue past the town centre on Peninsula Road for about 2km/1.2mi and turn R onto Coast Guard Drive you will encounter both the Amphitrite Point lighthouse and the Pacific Wild Trail that circles the point.

discoverucluelet.com

Surfers at Sea Lion Rock.

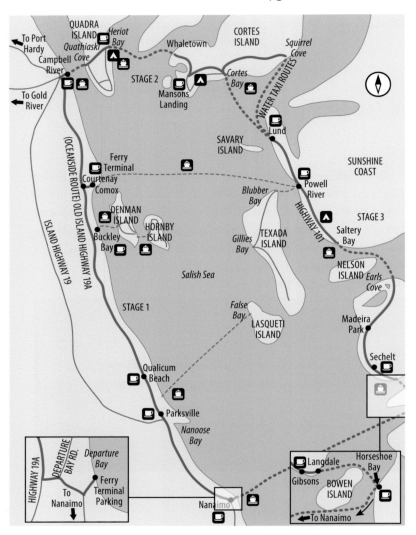

Tour of the Sunshine Coast

Although I've called this route the Tour of the Sunshine Coast, it has its start and first 150km/93mi along the east coast of Vancouver Island, hence its inclusion in this collection of Vancouver Island rides.

The loop route described below is a wonderful combination of oceanside riding, island-hopping and longish, scenic ferry rides. You can do the whole thing in three days or you can take a week, depending on your fitness level and time constraints. I've described the route in three stages, but as you will see, it's not difficult to modify each stage for your own purposes. (The route has its start in Nanaimo – at the Departure Bay ferry terminal to be exact.)

Once you leave Campbell River you're in another world. Travelling across Quadra and Cortes islands you get a taste of a more laissez-faire lifestyle where things move at a different rhythm – perceptible even though you're only passing through. You might be tempted to linger. If you do, the ferry schedules and availability of accommodation will no doubt set your agenda. The road across Cortes Island is hilly, so when you're making for the water-taxi pick-up at Squirrel Cove, make sure you give yourself plenty of time. (The water taxi will also pick up at the government wharf at Cortes Bay. Consult a map of the island for directions.)

The Sunshine Coast stretches from Desolation Sound in the north all the way down to Gibsons in the south – a distance of close to 170km/105 mi – and is known for its mild climate, its liberal smattering of coastal settlements and a collection of spectacular ferry routes that are the bane of residents but a delight for visitors.

The highlight of the tour is the 40-minute water taxi ride from Cortes Island's Squirrel Cove to Lund, a busy coastal village that caters mostly to the boating crowd. The craft can take six or more bikes and easily accommodates a dozen passengers. It's a nippy thing, its wake mesmerizing as you watch the islands of Desolation Sound recede behind you. If you're fortunate with the weather, you're guaranteed to have a smile on your face the whole way. (Make sure you book the taxi well in advance, at lundwatertaxi.com.)

Powell River is an old mill town that now relies on ecotourism and the arts as its main sources of revenue. It's also the ferry terminal for both the Texada Island ferry and the Comox/Powell River route.

The Saltery Bay to Earls Cove ferry route has to be one of the coast's most scenically pleasing. The 50-minute ride feels more like an exotic cruise than just travelling a transportation corridor, with the surrounding mountains of Jarvis Inlet towering over its deep-blue waters.

The longish ride from Earls Cove skirts four small seaside communities – Garden Bay, Madeira Park, Halfmoon Bay and Roberts Creek (all worth a visit) – before landing you in Sechelt, a name phonetically derived from the name of the First Nation of the area, the shíshálh.

The tour finishes with a little flurry: a steep descent into Gibsons Landing, a bustling little place made famous by the TV series *The Beachcombers*, and the undulating ride along Marine Drive to the Langdale ferry terminal.

(For a much shorter tour, pedal from Nanaimo to Courtenay/Comox to take the Comox/Powell River ferry and join the route at the beginning of stage 3, Powell River.)

With all the ferries on this tour, making sure you know the schedules beforehand will make your life much easier by avoid long waits, frantic dashes to catch a sailing, and unplanned and expensive layovers. Planning is everything.

bcferries.com

lundwatertaxi.com
sunshinecoastcanada.com
discoveryislands.ca

TOTAL DISTANCE	314km/195mi.
LEVEL	Moderate to strenuous.
HIGHLIGHTS	Oceanside riding; two island traverses; 40-minute ocean water-taxi journey; multiple ferry rides; ocean, island and mountain scenery.

STAGE 1: NANAIMO TO COURTENAY

Between Nanaimo and Courtenay you'll encounter a number of places that'll call out your name wanting you to stop. Rathtrevor Provincial Park is one. It's just before Parksville and has one of the Island's most impressive beaches. North of Parksville, Qualicum Beach has a roadside stretch of beach, as does Union Bay south of Courtenay. Also south of Courtenay are the islands of Denman and Hornby. Both have interesting parks and village centres and are a stone's throw away by ferry.

DISTANCE	105km/65mi.
START	The pay parking area of BC Ferries' Departure Bay terminal in Nanaimo. This area is to the R of the terminal's toll booths. The assumption is you drive to Nanaimo with your bike. If you're using public transportation, take the bus to downtown Nanaimo and pedal along the Old Island Highway to checkpoint 2 to start the route there.

The route

①   Leave the ferry terminal parking area on the one-way exit road on its east side. Keep R, following the signage for Parksville and Highway 19A.

After the first set of lights you climb Brechin Road up the highway.

② (1.5km/0.9mi)   At the top of Brechin Road, turn R after the traffic lights onto Highway 19A, aka Island Highway.

③ (31.5km/19.6mi)   Bear R to follow Highway 19A into Parksville. (This is also the start of the so called Oceanside Route.) The Inland Island Highway, aka Highway 19, starts here and veers L.

④ (104.4km/64.9mi)   Downtown Courtenay. You will have noticed signage for Highway 19A North/Campbell River on your way into town. Unless you want to bypass Courtenay itself or wish to go to the Comox/Powell River ferry terminal, keep straight.

To avoid stage 2 and reach the

A bluebird day at Qualicum Beach.

Comox/Powell River ferry at its Little River terminal from downtown Courtenay, ride north on 5th Street to about 750m/yd past the bridge and turn R onto Ryan Road (signed for the ferry). After 5km/3mi turn L onto Anderson Road. You now follow the signs for the ferry, 3km/2.8mi away.

STAGE 2: COURTENAY TO POWELL RIVER VIA CAMPBELL RIVER, QUADRA AND CORTES ISLANDS

The first few kilometres/miles of the journey to Campbell River is inland from the coast. But as you pedal farther north, the road starts to hug the shoreline. From Oyster River to Campbell River the waters of the Salish Sea are never far from view.

Depending how much time you have, Campbell River's visitor centre and art gallery on Shoppers Row are worth a visit and are just a stone's throw from the terminal.

Quadra is a large island, and along with Cortes and neighbouring islands it is part of the Discovery group. The We Wai Kai Nation's Nuyumbalees Cultural Centre is in Yaculta at the south end of the Island. To get there, turn R onto Green Road at the top of the ferry hill. It's about 3km/1.8mi away.

The lovely provincial park on Rebecca Spit is easily accessible off Heriot Bay Road shortly before the Cortes Island ferry terminal. Cortes Island's centre is in Mansons Landing, where there are stores and a museum. You'll miss this on the described route but it's an easy detour. Again, depending on your time, both islands are yours to discover. Good maps of the islands can be had at Campbell River's visitor centre.

DISTANCE	97km/60mi
START	The junction of 5th Street and Cliffe Avenue in downtown Courtenay.

The route

①   Follow 5th Street over the bridge to join the Old Island Highway (19A) going north out of town. (You will have passed Ryan Road a few hundred metres/yards back on your R. That's the road to the Comox/Powell River ferry terminal.)

② (24.7km/15.3mi)   Cross the Oyster River bridge and ride through the small community of Oyster River.

③ (38.2km/23.7mi)   Pass through the oceanside community of Willow Point and its collection of roadside wood carvings.

④ (45.2km/28.1mi)   Campbell River/Quadra Island ferry terminal next to downtown Campbell River. On entering the town, look for the ferry terminal sign and turn R after Robert V. Ostler Park, following the wide highway. The terminal is 100m/yd on your R.

                                    The ferry from Campbell River to Quathiaski Cove on Quadra Island runs basically every hour on the half hour from early morning to late at night. Check bcferries.com for the exact schedule.

⑤ (ferry to Quadra Island, 10 minutes)

                                    Once you're on Quadra Island the route to the Cortes Island ferry at Heriot Bay is very straightforward – you just follow the signs. There is one possible deviation: after a kilometre/0.6 mile, as Heriot Bay Road bears L to become West Road (the signed route to the ferry terminal) you continue on Heriot Bay Road to its end at the ferry terminal (Rebecca Spit is off this road). This is about 2km/1.2mi longer but a more interesting route.

⑥ (53.2km/33mi)   Ferry ride to Cortes Island, 45 minutes.

⑦ (arrive Whaletown, Cortes Island)
                   Leave the ferry terminal on the steepish Harbour Road. After 1.5km/0.9mi turn R onto Carrington Bay Road, signed for Mansons Landing, Smelt Bay and Squirrel Cove. After a further 1km/0.6mi, turn L onto Whaletown Road. Keep to Whaletown as it crosses the island to Squirrel Cove, a total distance of 15km/9.3mi from the ferry. In Squirrel Cove turn second L for the general store and third L for the government wharf where the water taxi docks.

⑧ (68.2km/42.4mi) Water taxi to Lund (approximately 40-minute crossing).

⑨ (Arrive Lund)   The road out of Lund is hilly and continues that way right to Powell River. The road is known as Highway 101 and the Sunshine Coast Highway.

⑩ (95.7km/59.5mi) Having descended a steep, winding hill and crossed the Powell River bridge, you pass through Powell River's historic district and make your way along Marine Avenue to the ride's end in what is known as Westview. This is where the ferry terminals for Comox and Texada Island are located.

STAGE 3: POWELL RIVER TO NANAIMO VIA SECHELT AND LANGDALE

This third stage of the tour is perhaps the most challenging in terms of terrain but it compensates by revealing some of the coast's unheralded and attractive small communities. Madeira Park and Garden Bay, with their hidden peninsula and mini lake district respectively, are delightful enclaves. Halfmoon Bay and Roberts Creek are other off-the-highway surprises. Sechelt is a lively coastal town, and the string of seaside communities south of it offer respite and refreshments.

At the southern end of the coast is Gibsons Landing, a small but appealing village, especially in the summer, with a selection of cafes and restaurants for tired and sweaty cyclists.

DISTANCE   112km/69mi

Bikes on the Desolation Sound water taxi.

The route

① Ride south along Marine Avenue. After 4km/2.5mi Marine becomes the Sunshine Coast Highway/Highway 101. The road is never far from the waters of Malaspina Strait, the part of the Salish Sea that separates Texada Island from the mainland, i.e., the Sunshine Coast. You will see Texada from time to time for the next 80km/50mi. It's a rather lumpy road but nothing horrendous.

② (31km/19.3mi) After a long downhill you arrive at the utilitarian but strangely picturesque Saltery Bay ferry terminal. The crossing to Earls Cove takes about 50 minutes.

③ (Earls Cove ferry terminal)

From the terminal you climb up to and along the shores of Ruby Lake. There are one or two beach accesses to the lake. The road now twists and turns and is rather lumpy (to say the least) as makes its way south. Just off the road after an hour or so of riding are the entrance roads to Garden Bay 8km/5mi away and, a little farther, Madeira Park.

At Halfmoon Bay (another settlement a little way off the highway) there is the possibility of a quieter route. If you turn R onto Redrooffs Road at the Halfmoon Bay welcome sign, you follow it through the small village to emerge back onto the highway 10km/6mi south. The highway route is 8km/5mi, a savings of 2km/1.2mi.

④ (85.0km/52.8mi) Enter Sechelt. In the summer this is a bustling place. There are ample amenities and it's a good place to regroup. South of here the road can get busy. However, as you enter Roberts Creek, if you turn R at a traffic light and the Roberts Creek fire hall (R) onto Roberts Creek Road, you can follow this, which becomes Lower Road at a three-way stop, and avoid the traffic of the highway. It rejoins the highway just before Gibsons.

⑤ (106.6km/66.0mi) In Gibsons, instead of turning L onto North Road to go to the Langdale ferry terminal, turn R onto School Road and descend a very steep hill into Gibsons Landing. At the bottom of the hill, after a stop sign, bear L onto Marine Drive and pass through the quaint village. Continue on Marine until you emerge at the Langdale ferry terminal to your R. It's a 5km/3mi ride from Gibsons to Langdale via this less travelled route.

⑥ (111.6km/69.3mi) Langdale/Horseshoe Bay ferry terminal. It's a 40-minute crossing from Langdale to Horseshoe Bay.

⑦ (Horseshoe Bay ferry terminal) After disembarking, follow the signs for cyclists and foot passengers to the exit. Purchase your ticket for Nanaimo's Departure Bay at the ticket booth at the entrance to the terminal. The ferry journey takes 1 hour and 40 minutes.

Davis Bay.

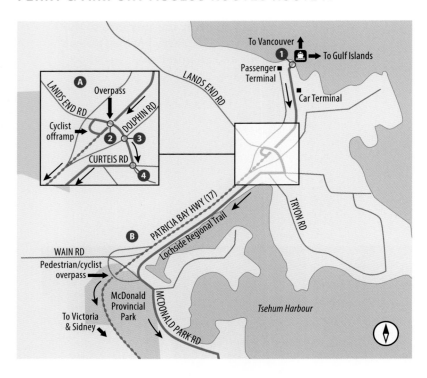

FERRY AND AIRPORT ACCESS ROUTES

Swartz Bay ferry terminal to Victoria

DISTANCE	32km/2omi
LEVEL	Easy

The route

① After walking your bike off the ferry, ride along the terminal's main exit road and either:
A: continue as the road becomes the Pat Bay Highway (17) to travel the 30-odd kilometres/16.5 miles on the highway's wide shoulder to Victoria; or
B: ride about 400m/yd and at 50m/yd past an overpass turn sharply R onto a well-marked bike path. (There is a good map of the suggested route into Victoria posted at this point.)

② Continue on this path for 50m/yd and turn R to ride over the overpass.

③ Ride through the traffic lights at the end of the overpass.

④ After a further 50m/yd, turn R onto Curteis Road and follow the Lochside Trail signs for 32km/2omi to Victoria.

NOTE: The Lochside Trail joins the Galloping Goose Trail at the Switch Bridge (which crosses the Trans-Canada Highway), with 4km/2.5mi remaining of your journey. The Johnson Street Bridge marks the end of the trail. You're on the edge of downtown Victoria now. Once you've crossed the bridge, if you turn R onto Wharf Street you'll find the Victoria visitor centre on your R where Wharf intersects Government Street (opposite the Empress Hotel).

Victoria to Brentwood Bay–Mill Bay Ferry Terminal

The ferry between Brentwood Bay on the Saanich peninsula and Mill Bay situated on the southern border of the Cowichan Valley provides us cyclists with a much quicker, less strenuous and decidedly quieter route to the roads, communities and attractions north of Victoria. Other than this ferry, the only viable way for most cyclists to ride north is on the Trans-Canada Highway up the long climb of Malahat Drive (apart from driving north with your bike in the vehicle). The ferry ride takes about 25 minutes and runs nine times a day (in both directions) throughout the year. Check schedules at bcferries.com.

DISTANCE	21km/13mi
LEVEL	Easy to moderate
START	The east side of the Johnson Street Bridge at the intersection of Wharf Street and Pandora Avenue.

The route (checkpoint numbers appear in red circles on combined map)

①   After crossing the bridge on the signed Galloping Goose Regional Trail, bear R onto Harbour Road for 400 or so metres/yards and turn R to continue on the "Goose" to its junction with Lochside Trail at the Switch Bridge.

② (4.0km/2.5mi) At the Switch Bridge turn L onto the continuation of the "Goose."

③ (5.0km/3.1mi) Cross traffic-lighted Tillicum Road, keeping to the paved trail. After

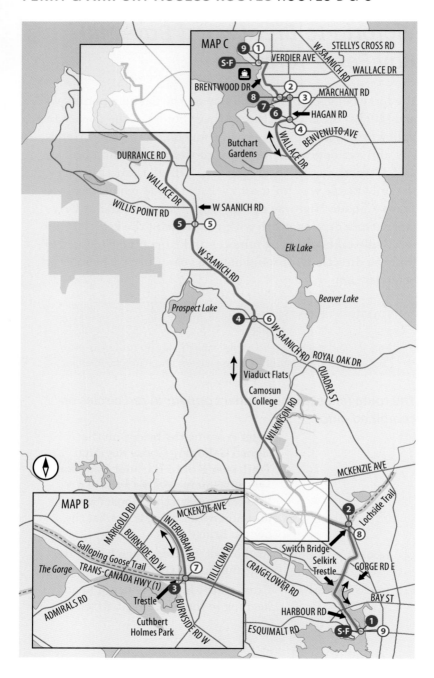

MAP C

STELLYS CROSS RD
W SAANICH RD
VERDIER AVE
WALLACE DR
S·F
BRENTWOOD DR
MARCHANT RD
HAGAN RD
BENVENUTO AVE
WALLACE DR
Butchart Gardens

DURRANCE RD
WALLACE DR
WILLIS POINT RD
W SAANICH RD
W SAANICH RD
Elk Lake
Beaver Lake
Prospect Lake
W SAANICH RD
ROYAL OAK DR
QUADRA ST
Viaduct Flats
Camosun College
WILKINSON RD
MCKENZIE AVE
Lochside Trail

MAP B
MARIGOLD RD
BURNSIDE RD W
MCKENZIE AVE
INTERURBAN RD
Galloping Goose Trail
TILLICUM RD
The Gorge
TRANS-CANADA HWY (1)
ADMIRALS RD
Trestle
BURNSIDE RD W
Cuthbert Holmes Park
CRAIGFLOWER RD
Switch Bridge
Selkirk Trestle
GORGE RD E
BAY ST
HARBOUR RD
ESQUIMALT RD
S·F

about 100m/yd and just before a trestle bridge, turn R down a marked short but steep trail and turn R again onto the bike lane of Interurban Road.

④ (11.5km/7.1mi) After passing through two sets of traffic lights and at the end of Interurban, turn L at the light onto West Saanich Road.

⑤ (15.0km/9.3mi) Just past a farmers market store on your L, turn L onto Wallace Drive. Be cautious here as you cross oncoming traffic on West Saanich Road.

⑥ (19.7km/12.2mi) About 600m/yd after having crossed Benvenuto Avenue (which is the access road to Butchart Gardens) turn L onto Hagan Road.

⑦ (20.2km/12.5mi) Turn L onto Marchant Road. Follow Marchant as it swings R to become Brentwood Drive.

⑧ (21.2km/13.2mi) At the end of Brentwood Drive, turn L onto Verdier Avenue and ride the short distance down to the ferry terminal.

Once you've disembarked from the ferry, ride the 200 m/yd up to Mill Bay Road and turn R. This road takes you to village of Mill Bay and the Trans-Canada Highway about 5km/3mi away.

Brentwood Bay ferry terminal to Victoria

This is a companion description for cyclists who want to take the Mill Bay–Brentwood Bay ferry back to Victoria.

DISTANCE	22km/13.5mi.
LEVEL	Easy to moderate
START	Brentwood Bay ferry terminal

The route (checkpoint numbers appear in white circles on combined map)

①   Exit the ferry terminal and after 100m/yd turn R onto Brentwood Drive.

② (0.5km/300yd)   Turn R onto Marchant Road.

③ (0.7km/400yd)   Turn R onto Hagan Road.

④ (1.4km/800yd)   Turn R onto Wallace Drive. Stay on Wallace, crossing Benvenuto Avenue (which is the access road to Butchart Gardens R) and Durrance Road.
Pass Willis Point Road R just before Wallace junctions with West Saanich Road.

⑤ (5.9km/3.7mi)   Merge R onto West Saanich Road. There's a farmers market on your R just past this junction.

⑥ (9.4km/5.8mi)   At the first set of traffic lights turn R onto Interurban Road. You now cross two sets of traffic lights.

⑦ (15.9km/9.9mi)   After the second set of lights and just before an overpass and at a crosswalk opposite the intersection of West

Burnside Road R, turn L up a steep but short trail to the Galloping Goose Regional Trail and turn L again. (This is a tricky turn off Interurban Road and needs to be anticipated 50m/yd before the turn. Give clear hand signals of your intent, as you'll likely be crossing oncoming traffic. Road markings will indicate where you turn.)

⑧ (17.9km/11.1mi)   When the trail forks, keep to the R to cross the Switch Bridge. There are numerous crossings along this section of the Goose, so be aware.

⑨ (21.9km/13.6mi)   Having followed the trail to its terminus at the Johnson Street bridge, turn R once over the bridge onto Wharf Street and enter downtown Victoria.

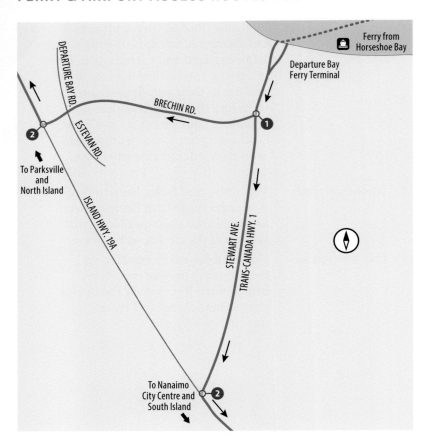

Departure Bay ferry terminal to Nanaimo/North Island*

Leave the ferry terminal by the exit road off the ferry's main car deck.

To Parksville, Courtenay and the North Island:

① (700m/yd)   At the first set of traffic lights, turn R onto Brechin Road. (This is signed for Parksville, Campbell River and highways 19 and 19A.)

② (1.0km/0.6mi)   After ascending the steep Brechin Road hill, pass through a traffic light and bear slightly L to climb about 50m/yd to another set of lights, at which you turn R onto the signed Highway 19A. This is the road to places north.

To downtown Nanaimo, Ladysmith, Chemainus, Duncan and the South Island:

① (700m/yd)   At the first set of traffic lights, continue straight on Stewart Avenue/ Trans-Canada Highway. This is signed for Nanaimo and Victoria.

② (2.7km/1.7mi)   As Stewart Avenue junctions Highway 19A at a traffic light, turn L to ride into Nanaimo, less than a kilometre/0.6mile away, and to places south.

* The other ferry from Vancouver to the mid-Island has its terminal at Duke Point, 16km/10mi south of Nanaimo. From there it's an

8.5km/5.3mi ride to Highway 1 (the Trans-Canada), where you then follow the signs for Victoria and south or for Nanaimo/Campbell River and north.

Victoria International Airport

For those arriving at Victoria International who want to cycle into Victoria, the following is the easiest route.

DISTANCE	28km/17.4mi
LEVEL	Easy

The route

① Exit the parking area and ride R past the airport's arrival doors. (The airport provides a sheltered bike reassembly facility located between the departure and arrival doors in the short-term parking area.)

② (400m/yd) At the first of three roundabouts, turn L (signed TO VICTORIA) and keep to the bike lane.

③ (1.4 km/0.8mi) Continue past the second roundabout.

④ (1.6 km/1.0mi) Willingdon becomes Canora Road.

⑤ (2.1 km/1.3mi) At the third roundabout, turn R and follow the paved path signed for the Lochside Trail. In following the path you'll cross the highway and an off-ramp on a pedestrian/bike overpass. (This may seem complicated but it isn't.) As you meet Lochside Drive/Trail turn R to ride the pleasant and relatively quiet 25km/15.5mi into downtown Victoria.

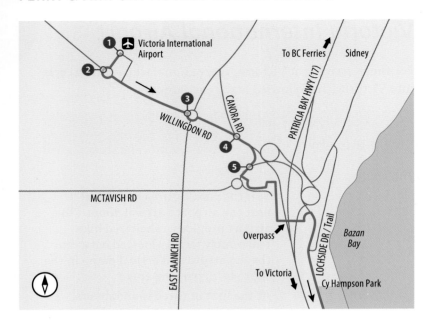

Index of Routes

About the Author

John Crouch has been cycling for most of his life, and the sport has become one of his abiding passions. He has toured extensively in Western Canada, including from Whitehorse, Yukon, to Victoria, BC; a five-day trans-BC tour; and exploring the back roads of southern Alberta. He has also toured through western Washington State, and once cycled from Victoria to San Francisco just to attend a friend's birthday. He has done all the long tours in this book more than once.

As a competitive athlete, John has won both the Canadian Masters long-distance triathlon and duathlon championships in his age group and the World Endurance Duathlon championship in the 60–64 age group.

John lives in Victoria with his wife, Lorinda. Besides riding his bike, he enjoys walking in his local neighbourhood and hiking in the hills surrounding the city.

He has written five other guidebooks: *Walk Victoria*; *Hike Victoria*; *Bike Victoria*; and *Cycling the Islands* as well as a cycling memoir titled *Six Highways to Home*.

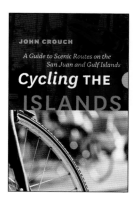

Cycling the Islands: A Guide to Scenic Routes on the San Juan and Gulf Islands

JOHN CROUCH

9781771601610

Featuring over 30 adventures on 11 different islands, each route includes a map and detailed information on local history, topography, aesthetics, places of interest, type of road, general route condition, level of difficulty, start and end points, checkpoints along the way and plenty of full-colour photographs. All of the text and accompanying information is fun, accessible, clearly laid out and easy to use.

Readers can escape to unique destinations in both Canada (Salt Spring Island, Pender Island, Mayne Island, Galiano Island, Gabriola Island, Denman Island, and Hornby Island) and the United States (San Juan Island, Lopez Island, Orcas Island, and Shaw Island).

Complete with detailed information for all travellers, John Crouch's unique guidebook is the perfect resource for anyone heading to these popular destinations.

Available from rmbooks.com or your favourite bookseller.

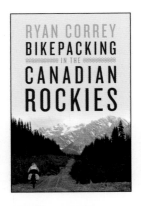

Bikepacking in the Canadian Rockies

RYAN CORREY | ROCKY MOUNTAIN BOOKS

9781771602372

Before his untimely death from cancer in 2018, veteran rider and passionate cyclist Ryan Correy (two-time finisher of the Tour Divide, founder of Bikepack Canada and author of *A Purpose Ridden*) pedalled his way through the most popular national parks in the Canadian Rockies in order to complete his work on this unique guidebook. Featuring routes in Waterton, Kananaskis, Banff, Kootenay, Yoho, and Jasper, *Bikepacking in the Canadian Rockies* will take biking enthusiasts on Beginner, Intermediate, and Expert journeys.

The result of Correy's remarkable dedication is an unparalleled collection of ten ambitious, multi-day routes complete with directional cues, detailed maps, a helpful Bikepacking 101 section, rich photography, and personal stories that will stoke the curiosity of both the beginner and the experienced backcountry rider.

Available from rmbooks.com or your favourite bookseller.

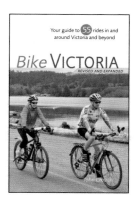

Bike Victoria — Revised & Expanded

JOHN CROUCH

9780973191349

In this revised edition of *Bike Victoria* you'll be introduced to eight new rides for your biking enjoyment. It will take you to places, trails, and roads you never knew existed.

Ride through Hazlitt Creek, along the Colquitz River, by Bear Hill, and explore the farther reaches of Thetis Lake Park.

Short urban rides are also here: the Coffee Shop Crawl and the Arborist's Ride will tempt you out on the dreariest of days.

No area of Victoria and vicinity is left out from this inclusive and extensive guidebook.

Available from bike-walk-victoria.com or your favourite bookseller.

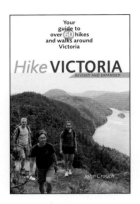

Hike Victoria

JOHN CROUCH

9780973191363

If you're one of those who enjoy being in the fresh air surrounded by the natural world, *Hike Victoria* is for you.

Within a stone's throw of the city you can be in the dense forest of East Sooke Park, on the ridgetop of Gowlland Tod, beside the placid waters of Matheson Lake, beachcombing on the shores of Island View Beach or strolling through a quiet neighbourhood in North Saanich.

Whether you want a vigorous hike or a pleasant walk, you'll find just what you want in this easy to follow and user-friendly guidebook.

Available from bike-walk-victoria.com or your favourite bookseller.

Walk Victoria — Revised & Updated

JOHN CROUCH

9780973191332

With eight additional walks and all the originals given a "face-lift," this new edition is an invaluable guide for exploring Victoria's diverse and scenic neighbourhoods.

Take a walk through View Royal's Portage Park or Gordon Head's Glencoe Cove–Kwatsech Park; stroll along the Uplands' gracious streets or visit Fernwood's Jewish cemetery; climb Fairfield's Moss Rock or discover Saanich's Old Joe's Trail – this detailed guidebook shows the way.

Find these and many more interesting walks in this new and extended edition of *Walk Victoria*.

Available from bike-walk-victoria.com or your favourite bookseller.